Alfred and Emily

ALSO BY DORIS LESSING

NOVELS
The Grass Is Singing
The Golden Notebook
Briefing for a Descent into Hell
The Summer Before the Dark
The Memoirs of a Survivor
The Diaries of Jane Somers:
    The Diary of a Good Neighbor
    If the Old Could . . .
The Good Terrorist
The Fifth Child
Love, Again
Mara and Dann
Ben, in the World
The Sweetest Dream
The Story of General Dann and
    Mara's Daughter, Griot and the
    Snow Dog
The Cleft

"Canopus in Argos: Archives" Series
Re: Colonized Planet 5, Shikasta
The Marriages Between Zones
    Three, Four and Five
The Sirian Experiments
The Making of the Representative
    for Planet 8
Documents Relating to the
    Sentimental Agents in the Volyen
    Empire

"Children of Violence" Series
Martha Quest
A Proper Marriage
A Ripple from the Storm
Landlocked
The Four-Gated City

SHORT STORIES
African Stories:
    Volume I: This Was the Old
        Chief's Country
    Volume II: The Sun Between
        Their Feet
Stories:
    Volume I: To Room Nineteen
    Volume II: The Temptation of
        Jack Orkney and Other Stories
The Real Thing: Stories and Sketches
    (U.S.), London Observed (U.K.)
The Grandmothers

OPERA
The Making of the Representative
    for Planet 8 (music by Philip Glass)
The Marriages Between Zones
    Three, Four and Five (music by
    Philip Glass)

POETRY
Fourteen Poems

NONFICTION
In Pursuit of the English
Particularly Cats
Going Home
A Small Personal Voice
Prisons We Choose to Live Inside
The Wind Blows Away Our Words
Particularly Cats . . . and Rufus
African Laughter
Time Bites

The Doris Lessing Reader

AUTOBIOGRAPHY
Under My Skin
Walking in the Shade

Alfred
and
Emily

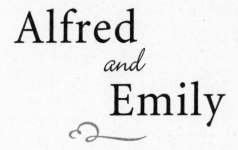

DORIS LESSING

HARPER

An Imprint of HarperCollins*Publishers*
www.harpercollins.com

Les

HarperCollins books may be purchased for educational, business, or sales promotional use. For information please write: Special Markets Department, HarperCollins Publishers, 10 East 53rd Street, New York, NY 10022.

First published in Great Britain in 2008 by Fourth Estate, an imprint of HarperCollins Publishers.

FIRST U.S. EDITION

Library of Congress Cataloging-in-Publication Data

Lessing, Doris May, 1919–
    Alfred and Emily / Doris Lessing. — 1st U.S. ed.
      p. cm.
    "First published in Great Britain in 2008 by Fourth Estate"—T.p. verso.
    ISBN 978-0-06-083488-3
1. Lessing, Doris May, 1919—Family—Fiction. 2. Lessing, Doris May, 1919—Family—Biography. 3. World War, 1914–1918—Casualties—Biography. 4. Amputees—Great Britain—Biography. 5. British—Zimbabwe—Biography. 6. World War, 1914–1918—Social aspects. 7. World War, 1914–1918—Psychological aspects. I. Title.
    PR6023.E833A78 2008
    823'.914—dc22

2008017453

08 09 10 11 12 OFF/RRD 10 9 8 7 6 5 4 3 2 1

FOREWORD

My parents were remarkable, in their very different ways. What they did have in common was their energy. The First World War did them both in. Shrapnel shattered my father's leg, and thereafter he had to wear a wooden one. He never recovered from the trenches. He died at sixty-two, an old man. On the death certificate should have been written, as cause of death, the Great War. My mother's great love, a doctor, drowned in the Channel. She did not recover from that loss. I have tried to give them lives as might have been if there had been no World War One.

Easy for my father. He grew up playing with the farmers' boys in the fields around Colchester. He had wanted to be a farmer, all his life, in Essex or in Norfolk. He did not have the money to buy a farm, so I have given him his heart's desire, which was to be an English farmer. He excelled in sport, particularly cricket.

My mother nursed the wounded for the four years of the war, in the old Royal Free Hospital, which was then in London's East End. When she was thirty-two, she was offered the job of matron at St George's Hospital, then one of the greatest hospitals anywhere. It is now a hotel. Usually women had to be in their forties to be offered matronhood. She was formidably efficient. I used to joke, as a girl, that if she were in England she would be running the Women's Institute or, like Florence Nightingale, be an inspiration for the reorganization of hospitals. She was also musically talented.

That war, the Great War, the war that would end all war, squatted over my childhood. The trenches were as present to me as anything I actually saw around me. And here I still am, trying to get out from under that monstrous legacy, trying to get free.

If I could meet Alfred Tayler and Emily McVeagh now, as I have written them, as they might have been had the Great War not happened, I hope they would approve the lives I have given them.

Alfred and Emily

PART ONE

Alfred and Emily: a novella

1902

The suns of the long summers at the beginning of the last century promised only peace and plenty, not to mention prosperity and happiness. No one remembered anything like those summer days when the sun always shone. A thousand memoirs and novels averred that this was so, and that is why I may confidently assert that on that Saturday afternoon in August 1902, in the village of Longerfield, it was a splendid afternoon. The occasion was the annual celebration of the Allied Essex and Suffolk Banks, and the place was a vast field lent every year by Farmer Redway who usually kept cows in it.

There were different focuses of activity. At the end of the field, excited cries and shouts told that here were the children's games. A long trestle table laden with every kind of foodstuff stood under some oaks. The main arena of attention was the cricket match, and around the white-clad figures clus-tered most of the spectators. The whole scene was about to be absorbed by the shadows from the big elms that divided this field from the next where the expelled cows watched the pro-ceedings, while their jaws moved reminiscently like those of gossips. The players in their fresh whites, which were a bit dusty after a day of play, knew their importance in this summer festival, conscious that every eye was on them, including those of a group of townspeople leaning over a fence, who were determined not to be left out.

Not far from the cricket pitch there were, sitting on the grass with cushions, a large, fair woman, whose reddened face said she did not enjoy the heat, a tiny shred of a girl, her daughter, and a girl who had just leaned forward, her eyes on Mrs Lane's face to hear what she was saying. 'It is a very serious thing, my dear, quarrelling with your father.'

At this moment, a youth was coming forward to stand with his bat at the stumps, and the fair woman leaned to send him a wave, which he acknowledged with a smile and a nod. He was strik-ingly good-looking, dark and well built, and that there was something especial about his standing there was shown by a sudden silence. The bowler sent down a ball and the batsman easily knocked it well away.

'Sssh,' said Mary Lane. 'Just a minute, I want to see …'

Daisy, the little girl, was already leaning forward to watch, and now Emily McVeagh, the other girl, watched too, though she was certainly not seeing much. She was flushed with excitement and determination, and kept glancing sideways at the older woman, hoping for her attention.

Another ball sped down towards the handsome youth, another prompt rebuff, and now there was a ripple of applause.

'Well done,' said Mrs Lane, and was ready to clap, but the bowler had begun his run forward.

Again … again … a ball came close to where they sat and the fieldsman ran to retrieve it. The innings went on, there were several scatters of applause, and then a burst of clapping when the youth sent a ball almost as far as the children's games.

It was time for tea. The long trestle table was besieged, while a woman stood by the urn and handed out cups.

'I could do with one, Daisy,' said her mother, and the girl ran to join the queue.

Now Mrs Lane remembered that very much more was being expected of her by the girl Emily, so she turned her attention to her and said, 'I don't really think you know yet what you are in for.'

Mrs Lane was a woman with influence, friends in useful places, and she had been finding out from a dozen different sources just what Emily McVeagh was in for.

The girl had defied her father, and said to him that, no, she would not go to university, she would be a nurse.

'She'll be a skivvy among skivvies,' Mrs Lane had said to herself, shocked at the girl's decision.

She knew John McVeagh well, knew the family, had watched Emily's triumphant schooldays with admiration tinged with regret that her daughter was not as clever and with as much presence and attack. The girls were friends, had always caused people to marvel at their unlikeness. One was retiring, easily overlooked, apparently frail, the other immediately mistress of herself and of circumstances, always first in everything, head girl at school, carrying off prizes: Emily

McVeagh, friend and champion of little Daisy.

'I know I can do it,' said Emily, calmly.

'But why, why?' Mrs Lane was wanting to ask, and perhaps would have done, except that the youth who had been earning applause came up to her and she leaned up to kiss him and say, 'Well done. Oh, well done.'

There was a little history here.

He accepted a cup of tea from Daisy, and a vast piece of cake, and sat down by his friend, Mrs Lane. She had known him all his life.

Two brothers: the older one, Harry, was adored by his mother. She was known to be discontented because her husband, the boys' father, a bank clerk and hating it, spent every moment of his spare time playing the organ in the church. Instead, it was clear, she felt, of trying 'to get on'. He was unambitious, but the elder son had been offered a job, much more than most schoolboys could expect, before he had even finished school. He, too, had been the clever one, easily passing exams, winning prizes. But this mother had not liked her second son, Alfred, or behaved as if she didn't.

Beating children in those days meant no more than an intention to listen to the wishes of God. 'Spare the rod and spoil the child.' But Mrs Lane, observing, had been shocked. She, too, was the wife of a bank clerk, a senior one, but her husband was a pillar of the Church, and involved with local activities. Alfred's misfortune in his mother had long been known, discussed, and the boy was given all kinds of indulgences and special favours from people who were sorry for him. If he was not interested in school, he was very good at games, particularly cricket. He had turned sixteen a week or so before, and he was too young to play in the men's game. But he was here, playing, and if Mrs Lane had had a good deal to do with persuading influential people that he should be given the chance to distinguish himself, then who would ever know it? Alfred's mother was sitting with the spectators, and when people congratulated her on her brilliant son she looked discomforted, obviously feeling that it was the other son who should always be applauded.

Alfred was being given a chance to show himself and his prowess and Mrs Lane was delighted with herself and with him. She had said often enough that she loved the boy as if he were her own, and she wished he were. She much disliked Alfred's mother, though in this community, everyone knowing the others, this was not something she could often express.

'Alfred,' she said, fanning herself with the programme of the day's events, 'Alfred, you've done us all proud.'

And now Alfred was being summoned from the pitch – and he hastened off, with smiles at the three, Daisy, who adored him, like her mother, and this other girl, to whom he had not been introduced.

Over on the pitch a little conference was going on, with Alfred, and while she watched this, Mrs Lane was again turning her attention to Emily.

'It is very badly paid, very, you have no idea,' said the older woman. 'You'll do skivvy's work, dreadful, and the hours are long. And the food is bad, too.' Another objection she did not find it easy to bring out. The girls who became probationers were the lowest of the low, she could have said, the roughest of working-class girls. And you, Emily McVeagh, have had an easy life, you've always had the best of everything, and you are going to find it very hard, very.

They were starting to play again, and the handsome boy was back at the wicket.

'If I understood why,' said Mrs Lane, coming out with it. 'If you could say why, Emily. You know, there aren't many fathers who want their girls to do university. He must be so disappointed.'

She did not much like John McVeagh, a pompous man, she thought, full of himself, but he was so proud of Emily, boasting about her everywhere in and out of season, so now he must be feeling ...

'He told me, "Never darken my doors again,"' said Emily, turning bright tear-filled eyes on her mentor. 'I wish she was my mother,' she had said often. This motherless girl, with an unkind stepmother, had made for herself a mother in Mrs Lane, who was now looking at her with deep disappointment. 'Do think, Emily, do think.'

But Emily was starting work as the lowest of the low, this coming week, at the Royal Free Hospital in the Gray's Inn Road in London. She could no longer stay at home: she had been formally thrown out.

'Never darken my doors,' she had heard. Repeating it now there was a satisfaction in it, as if in the repetition she was rolling her father, John McVeagh, out of her mouth, goodbye.

'He said I must not consider myself his daughter any longer,' she said, and it came out wildly, forlornly, and now the tears were running.

'My dear,' said Mrs Lane, putting her arm around Emily and kissing a cheek that was hot and wet with tears. 'But it doesn't matter what he says. You are his daughter and nothing and nobody can change that.'

From the cricket pitch came more applause. The handsome youth had been caught out, but obviously not disgracefully because he retired to join the spectators while people clapped. He was not surprised to see that his mother, who had been just there, watching him, had gone.

Mrs Lane, looking past Emily's head, also saw that the unkind woman, Mrs Tayler, had gone.

When Alfred came over to Mrs Lane, she let Emily go, to give him a hug, which said she was trying to make up for his mother.

'You did so well,' she said. 'Well done, Alfred.'

Alfred hesitated, saw that the girl whose name he did not know was crying and removed himself to a chair.

'Oh dear,' said the kindly Mrs Lane, again hugging Emily. 'Oh dear, oh dear, I wish I understood it.'

Alfred watched the cricket, but not so that he didn't hear the girl whose head was on Mrs Lane's shoulder say, 'I know it is the right thing for me. I know it is.' Alfred seemed to need to escape, but changed his mind and from the tea urn fetched more cups of tea, which he handed to the three women, with a bowl of sugar. As he gave her cup to Daisy, he asked, very low, 'Who is she?' and Daisy said, 'She's Emily,' as if nothing more need be said. 'She's my friend,' she added.

Oh, so that's Emily, Alfred thought, for of course he knew all about Emily, had heard so much. As often, faced with the reality of a real person – in this case a sobbing and dishevelled young woman – he was thinking that it was not easy to see, looking at her, why she meant so much to Daisy.

He was about to sit down again, his eyes already on the cricket, when his attention was drawn by a noise at the fence. The adults had gone on their way, but children were there now. Even from where he was, some yards away, it could be seen these were poor children. The girls were in raggedy dresses and bare feet. Some boys tried to climb the fence, their eyes on the trestle full of food.

'Take them something, Daisy,' said her mother. 'Take the sandwiches. I brought them,' she added, because the woman behind the tea urn was about to challenge her. Women, seeing the situation, were coming up to the trestle and Mrs Lane called out, 'Only what I brought, nothing else.'

Alfred and Daisy lifted plates of sandwiches and a couple of sponge cakes to the fence where the children snatched them. They were hungry.

The women who had arrived stood with tight lips.

'Only what I brought,' called Mrs Lane, smiling, but angry. She said under her breath, 'Their precious cakes are safe from me.'

'They are gypsies,' said one of the women. 'I wouldn't want my best sponge cake to go to them.'

'Well, even gypsies have to eat sometimes,' said Mrs Lane, and she was red with anger now.

'They are so poor,' said Alfred, frowning, speaking to Mrs Lane as if wanting an explanation. 'They look as if a square meal is what they need.'

'Yes,' said Daisy, smiling at the boy she had known all her life, the scrubby schoolboy who was suddenly a hero.

Emily was disengaging herself from Mrs Lane, retying the black ribbon that held her hair back. She was eighteen, her hair was 'up', but on this afternoon, with such old friends, the schoolgirl style seemed appropriate.

'I must go,' she said. 'I'll miss the train.'

'I'll go with you,' said Daisy at once.

Emily stood, smiling, blinking away tears. 'It is the first step that is the hardest,' she confided to Mrs Lane, taking command of her future, holding it safe from Mrs Lane's grave, silently protesting face.

The two girls went to the fence, Emily with her shadow Daisy just behind her.

At the fence she looked for a gate or aperture – nothing.

The children were hanging about, hoping for more.

Emily gave a quick flash of a glance around, vaulted the fence, and stood, smiling, victorious, back at Mrs Lane and the woman with the tea urn, who was shocked at this unladylike behaviour. No gate, so Emily lifted Daisy over, 'One, two, three,' and the two girls went off to the station.

Alfred was back with the group near the players.

Mrs Lane was now sitting in deep shade and her reddened

face was returning to its normal hue.

'It's all very well ...' she said, addressing perhaps some sparrows that were attacking the cakes. She thought of the girl's wonderful vault over the fence, the grace of it, the ease, and for some reason seeming to say no to Emily's rash and unthinking plan. 'Oh, no,' said Mrs Lane. 'Oh, no. It can't be. What a waste.'

August 1905

The scene is the same. The cows stand ruminating and watching. Alfred is batting. He is nineteen, and has been playing with the big men for two years. No nervous stripling now, no handsome boy, he is a young man and everyone is watching him, not only Mrs Lane, who is in a chair under her oak tree, fanning herself, and Alfred's mother, in tears that are intended to be seen.

If Mrs Lane's face shows varieties of ironic comment, then it is understandable.

On the day after we saw them all last, Daisy returned from London to say she intended to start with her friend Emily as a probationer at the Royal Free. Now it had happened, it was obvious that Mrs Lane could have foreseen it all. Daisy had always admired Emily, and had emulated her when her own talents would permit. Mrs Lane was shaken, shocked to the heart, and she could not stop weeping, until her husband, upset by his daughter, even more by her, called the doctor and told his wife, 'Now, my dear, that is really enough. You are taking it much too hard.' Mrs Lane did not know that anybody could weep as she was doing. Her little girl, whom she often privately called her little fairy, her little angel, was in that hospital wiping the bottoms of the very poor. That Emily had chosen to do it was dreadful, but she was at least a big strong girl, but her own little daughter, that frail child ... When a parent weeps and is inconsolable because a child does not go in the direction the parent wants, then at least one question has to be asked. Why is she so checked, so overthrown, as if given a death sentence, or at least part of her has? Or, for that matter, him: John McVeagh was ill with grief, so it was said.

And Mrs Tayler was noisily weeping over there, near the pitch, in a position where she had to be seen by everyone. Her Alfred, equably batting while people admired and applauded – he had been offered a variety of jobs by banks as far as Luton and Ipswich, not because of his aptness with the pen or with figures, but because they wanted him for their cricket teams. And he was good at billiards too, at snooker, at bowls – this young star was being competed for, his mother was as pleased as when her other son was chosen for his cleverness, but Alfred said, no, he would rather die than be a bank clerk, he had hated every minute of his two years in an Allied Essex and Suffolk bank. He was going to work for Mr Redway, the farmer who yearly lent his field for this festivity. Bert Redway was his good friend, they had grown up together; Alfred had in fact spent his childhood playing with the farmers' sons, along the hedgerows and in the fields.

'He's going to be a farmer's boy,' wept his mother. 'He's just like his father. They only care about making me miserable.'

And she had gone from kitchen to kitchen among the wives, complaining.

Alfred had only said, 'Mother, I am not going to be stuck in a bank, and that's the end of it.'

That morning he had emphasized his point by collecting the cow dung from all over the field, while the stewards, the supervisors of the children's games, the men who were making perfect the cricket pitch watched and grinned, or laughed, when the mother couldn't see. His father, briefly detaching himself from the church organ, had said, 'Well done, Alfred. I wish I could do the same.'

Mrs Lane was sorry for Alfred's mother, but convinced her own disappointment had to be worse. Alfred had been a farmer's boy all his life: nothing new about that. But that her little girl, Daisy … Mrs Lane sent to London every week a large fruit cake, a box of pies, all kinds of treats. Emily and Daisy slept in a room with six other probationers, scum from the East End, so Mrs Lane thought and said. The parcels did not have a crumb left in them ten minutes after they were opened: all the girls were hungry. The probationers had very little time off, and when Mrs Lane did see her daughter and Emily she was as shocked and grieved as she had expected. They were so thin, so exhausted. She had not exaggerated the hardships: she did not know how these gently brought-up girls survived.

She was expecting Emily to give in, apologize to her father, go home repentant. She did not. When Mrs Lane delicately enquired of her daughter if this might happen, Daisy said simply, 'But she couldn't do that. It's her pride, Mother.' And besides, Emily had never ever indicated that she felt she had made a mistake.

Pride, scorned Mrs Lane. It was stubbornness, it was sheer wrong-headed silliness. The girls' hands were rubbed red and raw, they both looked like skivvies; they *were* skivvies. That was all they did in their work, empty bedpans, scrub, dust, clean, wash floors, walls, ceilings, at it from dawn to dusk, and when they did get an afternoon off they fell on their beds and slept.

Mrs Lane told her husband she was so mortified she would die of it, but if she could have seen into the future … Her fairy child, little Daisy ended up as an examiner of nurses, and a steely glance from those spectacles dissolved many a poor examinee into tears. She was known as a strict examiner, but just of course, just, and fair.

Mrs Lane, who had longed for grandchildren, never did get any, for Daisy married, rather late, an eminent surgeon and was busy helping Emily with her charitable work.

But this afternoon, while feeling her heart would break, had broken, Mrs Lane banished any trace of tears and sat waiting for the girls, who had an afternoon off. She had checked that the food on the trestles was plentiful. She knew Emily and Daisy would fall on it the moment they arrived. She had already had words with the trustees of several hospitals, with well-known matrons and schools of nursing. It was wicked and short-sighted to expect girls to do such hard work on such poor food. She was planning a letter to *The Times*.

When the girls arrived, Mrs Lane would not allow herself to comment on how thin and bad they looked. They kissed her and at once attacked the food.

With laden plates they sat on cushions beside Mrs Lane and ate. Mrs Lane could not bear to look at those roughened hands: she literally averted her eyes.

'We cannot stay long,' said Emily and Daisy. They were both on night duty. Not probationers now, Mrs Lane had to remind herself. They were in their second year, were actually nursing patients. How time did fly, they all agreed.

Alfred, tea-time announced for the players, came over. He greeted Daisy, whom he had always known, but not Emily. He did not recognize her. He remembered Emily as a robust, tall girl – surely athletic: he had witnessed her leap over the fence.

He said to Mrs Lane, 'One reason I'm glad not to be going of to Luton or somewhere: I like dropping in for a bit of your fruit cake.' And his smile was certainly enough to win the heart of anybody at all who was not his mother.

'You know,' he said, 'I couldn't be in the bank. You know me.'

'Yes, Alfred, and I'm so glad you won't be going away.'

Daisy did not hear this, or pretended not to: she thought Alfred did not know she would be even more glad.

'Perhaps I'll drop in and see you when I come up to London,' said Alfred to Daisy.

'I'll look forward to it,' said Daisy.

Alfred was called back to the game; and soon the girls kissed Mrs Lane and went off back to London.

August 1907

Emily and Daisy passed their finals well, and Mrs Lane wrote to Mrs McVeagh, the stepmother. She had thought of writing to John McVeagh, but that would have been too much of a confrontation. The stepmother returned a note. 'Thank you for letting me know about Emily. What a clever girl she has always been. Yours sincerely.'

Mrs Lane was pretty sure John McVeagh would have been following Emily's progress, stage by stage. Mrs John McVeagh (that nasty old crow) had said 'letting *me* know'. Not one to go against her husband, then. Mrs Lane wrote to say she was giving a dance for her daughter, Daisy (whom of course they knew well as Emily's best friend), and for Emily. 'You would all be welcome.' The father and the stepmother wouldn't come, but there was Emily's brother. Perhaps he would.

Mrs Lane could have killed John McVeagh with her own two hands. Not to mention the stepmother. Surely they might have reflected that Emily had no one to applaud her, let alone make a dance for her. And could not that old stinge at least have given Emily money for some clothes?

On the nurses' pay Emily could not have afforded to dress well; she had the most basic of wardrobes. And she ought to have a dress, a real one: would it have cost that pompous old fool (John McVeagh) so much to send her money for a decent 'best' dress?

Emily would be dreaming of a dress, Mrs Lane knew. Her daughter was. Wouldn't any girl? Not since she was a schoolgirl had Emily owned a pretty frock.

She's got no mother, no mother, Mrs Lane reminded herself as she planned a special dress for Emily. She had bought a bolt of sweetly pretty sprigged white muslin and she made Daisy (her little angel) a dress cut from one she had had herself as a girl. Puffed sleeves, ribbons, a fichu of lace. Having seen Daisy in it, she at once cut one out for Emily, having got Daisy to make sure of measurements.

They all got dressed in Daisy's bedroom, Mrs Lane in her best grey satin, and Emily was disappointed, though she tried not to show it. Sprigged muslin, and she hated it.

Emily was strong, lean and well muscled, after the hard labour of nursing, and she was rather brown, having played a lot of tennis that summer. Emily dressed, knowing she looked gawky and uncomfortable. She thanked Mrs Lane, over and over again, because she knew that she loved her, and had done her best.

The bank was lending the Lanes their boardroom, all shining dark brown wood and heavy brown velvet curtains. In this austere setting Emily seemed even more out of place, with her little puffed sleeves and pink sash. Daisy looked wonderful.

Mrs Lane was dissolved in love for her little flower and sick with shame because she had done so badly for Emily. All the young men who worked for the bank as far as Ipswich were there, and some of the farmers. Daisy was dancing every dance, a veritable whirl of flowery muslin and smiles. The men were queuing up to dance with her, Alfred more persistent than anyone. This was a high point in Daisy's life and she never forgot it. She had passed her exams well enough, and now Alfred, her hero since she was a tiny girl, took her around the floor for dance after dance.

Emily did not do so well. Alfred did dance with her but she was awkward and stiff, probably because she hated how she looked.

A triumph, then, for Daisy, and something to forget as soon as possible, for Emily. That night, Emily wept silently in her bed, in Daisy's room, and Mrs Lane wept at what she had done, or not done for Emily, whom she loved so well. She cried until her husband stirred in his sleep beside her and asked her what was wrong.

Mrs Lane had made sure the local paper had sent someone to the dance, had instructed him in what to say, making a point of singling out Emily, and she sent the cutting to the McVeaghs.

Heartless, horrible people. Cold and heartless and horrible, imprecated Mrs Lane.

In the morning, Alfred opened the Lanes' kitchen door and saw Mr Lane eating his porridge at the head of the table.

'Oh, there you are, old son,' said Mr Lane. 'Porridge? Toast? The tea's just made.'

Alfred dropped in at this time most mornings. It was really to see Mrs Lane, though this morning he hoped he would catch Daisy before she left for London. He was always hungry: he had been up for hours. Today he was out by four. He had been thinking of Daisy, yes, but more on the lines of: I've known her all my life but only now do I really see her, what she is.

Alfred ladled himself porridge from the black pot that simmered all night on the stove, which was burning merrily, having been well stoked.

Mr Lane, a father as well as a husband, had been thinking of how Alfred had flirted with Daisy all evening and wondered if he could expect Alfred to ask for her hand. If so, what should he say? Daisy was doing so well, and did he, her father, want her to marry a farmer? I will deal with that when I come to it, he decided, and went on eating toast.

Meanwhile, in the bedroom, Daisy was singing as she brushed her hair, for she had been dreaming all night of handsome Alfred. But Emily, packing her case for London, could not bring herself to put into it the white frock that had caused her so much heartache. Mrs Lane saw her and came over and put her arms around the girl. 'I'm so sorry,' she whispered. 'If you only knew how ashamed I feel …'

'You are so good to me always,' said Emily, and saw with relief that Mrs Lane was going to take the frock – take it and, oh, burn it, hide it, I never want to think about it again.

Mrs Lane came first into the kitchen, greeted Alfred and said, yes, she would like some porridge.

Almost at once Daisy came in, and she and Alfred began joking and flirting. Alfred loved flirting, and it became so noisy and outrageous that Mr Lane had to laugh, and went out saying, 'Well, better you flirt with my daughter than with my wife, I suppose.'

And now entered Emily, and Alfred was thinking, Now, who is this bobby-dazzler, who can she be? And then immediately recognized Emily, who was as far from the flowery-muslin-frocked maiden as could be imagined. She wore a dark blue skirt, and a blouse of dark blue stripes that had a small white linen collar.

She smiled at Alfred, hoping he would not remember her as she was last night, and said she did not feel like eating. Some tea, perhaps.

Alfred thought she looked tired and sad: a contrast to the frivolity of the last few minutes.

He said to Daisy, but it would have been to Emily too, 'Shall I come and see you when I come to town?'

'Oh, yes, please,' said Daisy.

'Yes, do,' said Emily, being no more than polite.

'We will probably find a little flat for the two of us,' said Emily. 'We've had enough of nurses' quarters.'

'So check with Mother,' said Daisy, recognizing at that moment that her dreams of last night were only that.

And at this moment Bert Redway knocked on the open

door, pushed it half open and said to them generally, 'I've come for Alfred.'

This, too, happened most mornings.

Alfred gave a little half-mocking bow to Daisy, went around the table to embrace Mrs Lane, and to Emily said, 'Well, perhaps I'll see you when I do get up to town.'

He and Bert strolled off down the path. Bert had a hay fork over his shoulder, and from the gate Alfred picked up another from where he had left it.

The two young men went off, and Daisy and Mrs Lane were at the door to watch them.

'I love seeing Alfred with Bert,' said Mrs Lane. 'They are so good for each other.' She was not referring to Alfred's special position with the Redways – 'more of a son, really' – but that Bert tended to be wild, sometimes drank too much, and Alfred steadied him.

'Alfred's like an older brother to Bert,' said Daisy's mother, embracing Daisy as she went by.

'And it is time we left,' said Emily.

Again Mrs Lane stood to watch two young people go off, but in the opposite direction to the men.

The Best Years

And now Emily and Alfred were at the top of their lives, their fortunes – of everything.

'If only we could live our good years all over again,' my mother would say, fiercely gathering those years into her arms and holding them safe, her eyes challenging her husband as if he were responsible for their end.

'Yes,' he would say. 'What good times they were. Oh, what jolly times we did have.'

Alfred, on the Redway farm, was where, really, he had been all his life. From a tiny boy he had played with the farmers' sons and over the farms. The ditches, the hedgerows, the fields were his playground, and Bert had been his especial friend, as he was now. The two young men were at work, supervising the hired men, or on their own until the light went every night, when Albert went with Bert to the pub – certainly a chief responsibility – and then home with him to supper. He lived in the Redways' house, like a son. Alfred liked to look after the beasts; Bert supervised the crops. All summer weekends Alfred was playing cricket, and he competed in billiards and snooker matches. Bert liked going to the races, and Alfred tried to go with him, if there was time, for the big, ruddy, good-natured man with his black curls and loud laugh was known for his affability and, too, his tendency to get much drunker than an occasion needed. Alfred often took the tankards out of Bert's hands and got him home before too late. He knew that Bert's parents relied on him for this.

He loved to dance, too, and if there was a dance big or small anywhere around on a Saturday, he might walk to it, several miles, and walk back, through the early morning.

Alfred's life was, then, hard work and hard play, but because of Mrs Lane, who belonged to a travelling library, he read a good bit. Bernard Shaw, H. G. Wells, Barrie – he discussed them with Mrs Lane, and with Mr Lane, who liked politics too. 'I am a true blue Tory,' Mr Lane announced, partly to tease his wife, who had socialist and pacifist leanings. Alfred visited the Lanes when he could for the sake of some debate and to borrow books and magazines.

He went up to London for the music-hall, which he loved, and for plays. He might drop in on 'the girls', as Mrs Lane called them. 'Do go see the girls, Alfred, and come and tell me how they are.'

The 'flat' they lived in – called that because it was modish, not to say quite daring, still, for girls to live in a flat and keep themselves – was really two rooms at the back of a workman's house near the hospital.

'I did like going to have supper after the show,' he would reminisce, years, decades, later. 'Oh, it was such fun, at the

Trocadero, at the Café Royal.' But then there was the problem of catching the last train back to Colchester. More than once he dossed down on the floor of the girls' living-room, but the woman of the house, Mrs Bruce, said she did not like a young man sleeping in unmarried girls' rooms.

'But, Mrs Bruce, I've known them all my life,' said Alfred; 'they might be my sisters.'

'But they aren't your sisters, as far as I can see,' said Mrs Bruce, lips thin, arms held tight over a bossy bosom. 'I simply don't like it.' And she would wait till he came in, the girls being there or not, and open the door suddenly, without knocking …

'Mrs Grundy,' apostrophized my father, years and decades later. 'Mrs Grundy', an exemplary moral lady, is to be found in novels and memoirs of the time. Who was she? 'Mrs Bruce was like my mother,' said Alfred, even as an old man – well, as old as he got. 'Never say a nice thing if you can say a nasty one. Mrs Grundy sees dirt and filth where anyone else sees a nice clean floor.'

Alfred did see Emily on his London visits, but not often. Daisy was more often in than Emily, and she would apologize.

'You know Emily,' she would say, 'she's such a goer. Often I hardly see her myself for days. She blows in and blows out. Well, rather like you do.' For Daisy would have been happy if Alfred came more often and stayed longer.

If Emily was a 'goer' then was not he?

'If only I had Emily's energy,' Daisy would mourn. 'Where does she get it from?'

'For goodness' sake,' Mrs Lane might say, 'sit down a minute, Alfred. Have a cup of tea. Look, here's some of my cake that you like.'

'The pigs need moving ... I've got a cow due to calve, and it's time to get the beet in off the top field,' Alfred might say, while she put her two hands on his shoulders and pushed him into a chair.

'I never see you enough, Alfred. And Daisy doesn't seem to have time these days. As for Emily – perhaps she'll come for the big day next month.'

And perhaps not.

'How did we do it?' my father might demand of my mother, looking back at his youthful self. 'Good God, when I think ...'

'God knows,' says my mother, sighing. 'I was never tired in those days.'

Emily, Sister McVeagh at the Royal Free, loved her work.

'A bit of a martinet, but she was always fair.' This was Daisy, who was working her way along a different itinerary.

Emily played tennis with schoolfriends to whom she was writing in her old age: 'Do you remember ...'

She worked hard at her piano and took her finals in that time. The examiners told her she could have a career as a concert pianist if she wanted. She played the organ for services at All Souls, a fashionable church in Langham Place. She played concerts, recitals, and for social events at the hospital, even for nurses' dances. A good sport, was Sister Emily McVeagh.

During those years a message came from her stepmother

that she thought her father would like to see her.

Not from her father himself, though.

Emily went to lunch at her old home. Perhaps she went more than once.

'But I never forgave him, never, never,' she would insist, eyes flashing, her hands in fists.

What would 'forgiving' him have meant, from a daughter who had disobeyed him, was independent, doing very well, surely an ornament to him, the family – everyone?

'Father, thank you, I owe you so much.' Yes?

Well she certainly did owe him a lot.

'Without you I never would have …'

Possibly true.

But she couldn't forget those early years as a nurse. 'It was so hard, it was so difficult' – and she was not talking about the sheer hard labour of the beginning nurse's life.

'I was so hungry. We all were. I couldn't even afford to buy a decent pocket handkerchief,' she appealed, tears in her eyes. 'The pay was so bad. I couldn't even buy a pair of gloves,' said my mother, to a girl who was usually out in the bush some-where, dusty bare legs in *veldschoen*, in a frock run up from a reduced dress length from the store, with scratched hands, because the sitting hen didn't like being handled, or I had been climbing over a barbed-wire fence. *Gloves!*

'I couldn't buy some nice gloves. Even a tiny bit of an allowance … a little pocket money.'

When my mother went into Banket on mail days, she wore a proper hat, its ribbon always kept new and smart, white gloves that had little buttons, and her shoes were polished. In her handbag was a fresh white linen handkerchief. Her dress would be the 'tailored' dress that all the women of the district wore for special occasions. She could have walked down the main street of any big city.

But would she have taken an allowance from her father? I think not.

Emily didn't like dancing much, concerts and the theatre were what she liked, but Daisy asked Alfred up to a Christmas dance for the senior nurses, and there he danced all evening with one Betsy Somers. She was a small, plump girl with fair hair in curls and little ringlets, and cheeks that mottled easily when it was hot. Knowing people pointed out to each other that Betsy was very similar to Mrs Lane.

Getting married – now that was a big step, surely?

Mr Redway was a kind man and Alfred earned a good bit more than a labourer, but it wasn't enough to marry on. And he could hardly ask Betsy to live in the Redways' house.

That Alfred was going up to London as often as he could to see a nurse became known, and Mr Redway said to Alfred that he would accompany him to the top field to look at the new cowshed.

Alfred wondered what was coming: probably Bert's drinking.

The Redways' house had once been the manager's house for a large estate that had done badly and was divided and sold. As well as the Redways' house there were a lot of cottages, of various kinds and sizes, which had in them the labourers and their families. To the side of the top field was a little wood, where Mr Redway stood with Alfred and said he planned to build a fair-sized house just there. 'Of course,' said Mr Redway, 'Bert could live in it, but I'd rather he was at home.' Alfred understood. His conversations with Mr Redway were like this: most things left unsaid. Bert was a fair old trouble, these days, and Alfred could not be expected to live with him and look after him. 'If you want to get wed,' said Mr Redway, 'you can have the house, and I'll see you right.' Here, what could have been said was something on the lines of, 'I wish you were our son, Alfred. I could leave the farm to you, without a moment's worry about it. But you aren't, and so we must make the best of it. If Bert were thinking of getting married, then ... but he doesn't seem to have plans.' Aloud: 'Betsy Somers, hey? Isn't that a Kentish family? Why don't you bring her down for the weekend? Perhaps for our annual do. Does Betsy like cricket?'

'I hope so,' said Alfred, laughing. 'She's going to have a bad time of it if she doesn't.'

That was how Alfred's future was decided. And Alfred liked to think of Betsy sitting in a chair beside Mrs Lane, watching him play.

And what had not been said aloud? 'You must see we want to look her over. Is she going to fit in with us?' And so it goes always with a well-settled community when a son is bringing in a bride. *Will she become one of us?*

'Are you going to want thatch or slates for the roof?' said Mr Redway.

'Slates,' said Alfred. 'Better for fire.'

He would ask Betsy to marry him, when the house was done, but there was no hurry. He thought he probably loved her, but his life as a bachelor was really so very pleasant. And then Fate took a decided turn. He was up in London, and actually in the girls' flat, having supper, when a pain in his side felled him groaning to the floor. They were walking distance from the Royal Free. Daisy ran to the hospital and brought porters and a stretcher while Emily was taking Alfred to the front door. Off he was whisked to an operating theatre, just in time to save his life. His appendix had burst. He was in hospital long enough for him to decide that, yes, he really did love Betsy. They were engaged to marry. Meanwhile, Emily McVeagh announced her engagement to Dr Martin-White from Cardiology. There was a small party, in the office of Sister McVeagh's ward. Alfred was there, on crutches, in a corner, watching, with Daisy. Betsy was on duty somewhere.

'He looks a really nice chap,' approved Alfred to Daisy.

Dr Martin-White was very different from the people Alfred was surrounded by most days, all farmers, labourers, country people. He was tallish, perhaps too thin, with a hesitant manner, as if he felt he presumed, with a thoughtful, sensitive face.

This happened in 1916.

In life, my father's appendix burst just before the battle of the Somme, saving him from being killed with the rest of his company. He was sent back to the trenches where shrapnel in his right leg saved him from the battle of Passchendaele. 'A pretty lucky thing,' he might say. But, later, 'That is, if you set so much store on being alive.'

Now things moved fast. Betsy said she would not mind missing the last year of her training, if that meant she could marry her Alfred now. Alfred, who had imagined getting married at a quite comfortable time ahead, heard Betsy say she could not bear to be separated from him, and found himself agreeing with her. 'Why wait?' she said, and then so did he. But where were they going to live? Their house was nowhere near being finished. So, after all, that meant they would start married life in the Redways' house. And meant, too, that the looking-over of Betsy could not be postponed. 'Of course they have to give me a good looking-over,' she said, confident that this would go well: Betsy knew people liked her, so why not the Redways? But Alfred was more concerned that Mrs Lane should meet her, and at once. If Mrs Lane did not approve, then ... Would he be prepared to give up Betsy? The question did actually present itself to Alfred, and forcefully. No, he wouldn't. And that was how Alfred learned that Betsy was indeed essential to him.

No one need have worried. Mrs Lane, expecting her favourite Alfred's chosen, stood by her window, waiting. At the gate stood a plump fair girl 'all of a tremble', as Mrs Lane described it to Alfred. Mrs Lane ran down to the gate and embraced Betsy. 'Oh, welcome, dear Betsy,' crooned Alfred's other mother. ('She's been more a mother to me than my own ever was.')

The women wept in each other's arms and Mrs Lane told Alfred he was a lucky man. 'She's lovely, Alfred. Oh, well done.'

At the Redways, at once a difficulty. Bert came in from the pub because Alfred's fiancée was coming to supper, and he took to her at once, but showed it by teasing and needling, sometimes not very pleasantly, because he was half tight.

She stood up to him well, while her soon-to-be 'father-in-law and mother-in-law' watched silently, and gave her good marks.

Bert said to Alfred that he was a lucky dog.

And when the Allied Bank's annual beanfeast came around again, Betsy was sitting beside Mrs Lane under the oak tree, applauding when Mrs Lane indicated she should. There was a pretty good crowd that afternoon, because Alfred Tayler was there, and for the first time Betsy saw her Alfred in his element.

There were two celebrations for Alfred and Betsy's marriage, one a real wedding in Kent, where Alfred was surprised to find he was part of a large and amiable family. He would always like other people's families better than his own. Emily did not go – she was busy with her new home. Daisy went, and Mrs Lane. There was to be another party for the two, to be given by Mrs Lane, when the harvest was in. Meanwhile an invitation arrived to Emily McVeagh's wedding, for Betsy and Alfred. It was a large, elegant invitation on card as fine as best china, and it stood on the breakfast table at the Redways', and at the sight of it Bert took off into a rage. He had been bad since Betsy came, drinking more, and unpredictably emotional about everything. 'Just you look at that,' he jeered. 'And who the hell does Emily McVeagh think she is? Lady Muck, that's what she is.'

Now Bert had not much noticed Emily before, probably he had scarcely known who she was. Now he went on, 'Marrying in that church, is she? And I suppose you are going to trot off like a good little girl to the wedding.'

Betsy said equably, 'Bert, I've known Emily for years. I was a probationer in her ward. I was under her for my training. she was good to me. Some of those sisters were real bullies, so I was lucky to get her.'

'Sister McVeagh into Lady Muck,' shouted Bert. And he bowed clumsily, where he sat, a sort of obeisance, knocking over the toast in its rack.

'Steady on,' said Mr Redway. 'I liked Emily McVeagh. She used to visit Mary Lane.'

'Well, she won't be coming now,' said Bert. 'She'll be too grand for that. St Bartholomew bloody Church, and the reception at the Savoy.' And he grabbed the invitation, apparently about to tear it.

Betsy took it from him, and said, 'Bert, Emily is my friend. Please remember that.'

'Remember it!' shouted Bert. 'I expect you'll be reminding us often enough of your grand friends.'

Here Mrs Redway, who kept a sick headache in store for such occasions, rose to her feet, murmuring, 'My head …' and left the room.

'That's enough, Bert,' said Mr Redway.

'And I suppose Alfred won't be grand enough for you now,' said Bert.

And Betsy, who was usually good for much worse 'teasing' from Bert, burst into tears and went to the bedroom.

Mr Redway was white with anger. 'I've never been more ashamed ...' And he walked out.

Alfred said, 'And now, Bert, it's time you stopped all this.' He was probably thinking that 'all' included his drinking. But Bert was not drunk. He had, however, reached that stage when a glass of water or a cup of tea could trigger off the drunkenness of the night before.

'I'm getting tired of it, Bert. When it comes to making Betsy cry, then that's enough.'

'But I was only teasing,' said Bert, really upset, both by his father's going, and by Alfred. 'I was just joking, that was all.'

'I don't know how often these days I have to comfort Betsy when she cries because of you.'

'You're making a fuss about nothing,' blustered Bert.

'Bert, if you can't stop goading Betsy I'm going to take her to live at the Lanes' until our house is done.'

'You can't do that ... you wouldn't do that ...' And now Bert was really shaken.

'Yes, I will,' said Alfred. 'Listen, Bert, just listen ...' And Alfred leaned forward, grabbed Bert by the shoulders, to make him listen. 'Betsy is my wife,' said Alfred. 'She has to come first.'

Bert, shocked, was ready to cry himself. 'But, Alfred, you wouldn't ... you couldn't.'

'Yes,' said Alfred.

'But it's not as bad as that,' said Bert. 'It's simply not …'

'You make her cry and I have to tell her you don't mean it, but now it's enough.'

'But I love Betsy,' said Bert. 'I don't make her cry, I just tease her a little.'

'Well,' said Alfred, looking Bert hard in the face, 'and *I* love her, and she's my wife.'

Bert said, 'But you've only known her a little while.' And then, because of the absurdity of it, he went red and said, 'I'll say I'm sorry,' and he rushed to the bedroom Betsy had taken refuge in, knocked, and ran in. Betsy was crying on her bed.

'Betsy,' Bert shouted at her. 'Betsy, I'm sorry. I'm a clumsy brute. I'm so sorry, Betsy.'

Alfred waited a few minutes, then pushed the door open. Bert was kneeling on the floor by Betsy, his head on her lap. It looked as if he might be asleep. Betsy gestured, 'Rescue me …' And Alfred went to Bert, lifted him, saying, 'Now, come on, old son, that's enough.' And he put his arm around Bert and steered him out of the room.

'Thank you,' he heard from Betsy, as the two left.

Betsy and Daisy were to be bridesmaids at Emily's wedding, and today was the day Betsy was to go up to London for a rehearsal and to fit her dress.

She was to go with Mrs Lane, who was matron of honour.

Soon Betsy came out of the room, dressed for London, and the two men were still at the breakfast table.

She did not look at Bert, but said to Alfred, 'I'm leaving

now. Perhaps you had better not come.' Bert had been weeping, the sick, self-pitying tears of the alcoholic: it looked as if Alfred had been giving him a real talking-to.

Alfred had been going to London with her: Betsy, Alfred and Mrs Lane, a festive little party.

Outside the house Mr Redway was standing, apparently waiting for her.

'I'll go with you,' he said.

Betsy and her father-in-law proceeded up the path, which soon became a muddy lane.

When they reached the rutted mud, Mr Redway said, 'Hold on, I'll carry you across.' He put a large arm around the girl and lifted her, not only for the ten yards or so of the bad part, but until there was no mud. He set Betsy down gently and said, 'Don't mind Bert. He's not so bad, really. And I think your Alfred will sort him out.'

Betsy was grateful, and said, 'Thank you. I'm silly to get so upset.'

Meanwhile Bert had said to Alfred, 'You are going to stay with me? You aren't going to London?'

'No, I'm staying with you,' said Alfred. But he was wondering how much of this kind of adapting to Bert's weaknesses he must expect in the future.

'Come on, let's go and have a look at the corn, Bert.'

Bert did not again mention Emily, or the wedding. Alfred would have gone with Betsy to London for the occasion, but when the day came he again said to Bert that he would not go: he would stay. Mr Redway observed this and said, 'It's good of you, Alfred.' And he too went to where Alfred and Betsy's house was being built. Bert, Alfred and Mr Redway stood watching the builders, making suggestions, and Bert said suddenly, 'Betsy looked very nice in that dress.'

'But that's not what she'll wear for the wedding,' said Alfred.

Bert seemed to be about to explode again, in anger, reproach, accusation.

Mr Redway said, 'Just think, Bert. What's all this about? Emily McVeagh is getting wed. That's it. That's all.'

And that was why Alfred never got to Emily's wedding.

But the trouble was, if Emily had wed, Bert had not. More than once people had teased him that he was on his way to the altar, but then it all came to nothing. He took to doing his courting where his family and Alfred could not see, but last week, a girl he really did like, when he was taking her home from a dance, saw him fall down, and then watched him being very sick. She told him this was not how she visualized her future – Alfred knew about it, but not the parents, and Bert begged him not to tell them.

'They've been going on at me about getting married, but you don't seem to find it difficult.'

Now he had followed Betsy with his eyes, smiled when he looked at her, not knowing that he did, and Betsy told Alfred, 'He's just like Rover.' This was Mr Redway's big black dog, which adored her.

Then Betsy was being sick, and pregnant, and the doctor began joking that she must be having twins. She was large very early, and now it was a question of whether the house would be ready in time for the birth.

'I hope it will be. We don't have room here for a child,' moaned Mrs Redway, as if Bert had not been brought up in what was a pretty sizeable house.

When Bert returned in the evenings, drunk, Betsy scolded him, and he made excuses, and then one morning, entering the kitchen for breakfast, he had a scarlet weal on his cheek: apparently he did not know it. And now Betsy, seeing it, began to cry and said, 'Oh, Bert, you have to stop, you must,' while Bert dabbed at his cheek and succeeded in springing the blood, which ran. Betsy ran around to staunch the blood with her napkin while he joked and said it was worthwhile getting a bit of a scar, as she fussed over him.

'It's not funny, Bert,' she said. 'I've seen this before, with my cousin Edward. He was a drunk like you and he wouldn't stop and then he left the haycart brakes off and the cart ran back and killed him.'

Mrs Redway was tittering and gasping. She had watched her son descend through states and conditions of drunkenness but apparently decided not to notice it.

'Oh, Betsy,' she moaned. 'Bert isn't … he isn't …'

'Yes, he is,' said Mr Redway. 'And she's right, Bert, you have to stop.'

'Or you'll be like my uncle George,' said Betsy. 'He drank himself to death a couple of Christmases ago.'

'Betsy has an unlimited number of relatives who can be moral lessons to all of us,' said Alfred.

'Well, yes, I have,' she said. 'That's one good thing about being a member of a large family. And I'm sorry for you, Alfred. Not being.'

'Well, there's my brother,' said Alfred. 'But I am sure he never drinks anything but champagne.'

'Champers is no good,' said Bert. 'It gives you a headache.'

'I wasn't joking,' said Betsy. She didn't like Alfred's snooty brother. 'And there's my brother, Percy. No one ever says he's a drunk, but he is. On the way to the DTs,' said Betsy.

Now Alfred began laughing, and choked.

'Oh, Betsy,' he said.

Bert, relieved at the laughter, laughed too, and Betsy said sharply, 'It's not funny. If you don't stop, Bert, you'll be dead before you know it.'

Alfred laughed again and Betsy ran out of the room, crying.

'That's a shame,' said Mr Redway. 'You mustn't tease her, in her condition.' Betsy came back, eyes red, and Mr Redway got up and took her to the chair. 'You are quite right, Betsy,' he said.

'And now I'm going to finish saying my piece,' said Betsy. 'When my uncle George got so bad, he went to a man in London. He's a famous doctor, and that's where you must go too, Bert.'

Bert, seeing that he was cornered, said, yes, he'd go one of these days.

'No,' said Betsy. 'I'll take you. I'll get the address from my mother and I'll write and make an appointment.'

And she did.

On the day of the appointment it was very hot, and she was flushed and uncomfortable, but she said to Alfred, 'No, I'll take him. If you go with him he'll give you the slip and find a pub. He's afraid of me, you see, but not of you.'

'Afraid of you?' said Alfred. 'Who could be?'

'You'll see,' said Betsy.

Mr Redway said she could ride to the station on the old white mare, but Betsy said she wouldn't enjoy the motion of the horse. She would walk.

They set off, Mr Redway, Alfred, Bert and Betsy, along the dusty rutted lane to the station.

Betsy was looking quite sick with the heat, but she said, 'Don't fuss. I'm all right. And this is important.'

She bribed the guard to find a coupé and she and Bert got on.

Alfred and Mr Redway watched the train pull away.

'Well, Alfred,' said Mr Redway, 'you've got a prize girl there.'

'Yes,' said Alfred. 'I know.'

In London Betsy put her arm through Bert's and said, 'And now, Bert, you're not to go running off for a drink.'

Bert, who had been planning just that, said, 'I promise.'

At the doctor's in Wimpole Street, Betsy told the receptionist that this was Mr Redway and she had made an appointment for him, and she took him by the arm into the waiting-room.

'I say, Betsy, aren't you riding me a bit too hard?'

'No. This has to be done, Bert.'

When the receptionist called them, Betsy took him to the

doctor's door, saw him in, and then sat down heavily in the waiting-room: she really was feeling knocked out.

But she had her eye on the doctor's door and ran to it when, after a good long time, more than an hour, it opened. She received Bert, smiled at the doctor, said, 'I was the one who wrote to you.'

'And a very good letter it was,' said the great man.

Down in the street, Bert saw that Betsy was scarlet and sweating, and he called a taxi and helped her into it.

And still she held him tight by the arm, and all the way to the train, and again found the guard and gave him money for a coupé.

The guard was more alarmed about Betsy than about Bert, who was sober today.

At the station the other end were Mr Redway and Alfred, and with them holding her arm on either side, they set off home through the lanes that smelled of may blossom.

'Oh, that smell,' said Betsy. 'It makes me want to be sick.'

But she held out, got home, and went to lie down.

It was supper-time.

Mrs Redway, in her most suffering, gasping voice, at once demanded to know what the doctor had said. It seemed she imagined she would hear, 'Nothing much.' But Bert said, 'He told me if I didn't stop drinking I would be dead in ten years.'

Mrs Redway dabbed her eyes, moaned, 'Oh, no,' and seemed as if she would faint.

'And so, Bert,' said his father, 'that's it. You've got to do it.'

The supper ended. Bert went out to the side of the house

where there was a bench. Alfred followed him, at Mr Redway's look. He was afraid he would have sneaked off to the pub, but Bert sat on the bench in the late sunlight. Alfred sat by him and Bert said in a low voice, 'It's made me think, Alf. I really didn't believe it was as bad as that.'

'You've been pretty bad,' said Alfred.

Bert slumped there, shifted his feet about, sighed, coughed, and sent glances at Alfred.

'No,' said Alfred. He was finding this gaoler role hard: an easy-going chap, he was, and now he faced months – years – of saying, 'No, Bert. No.'

After a while Bert said, 'I'll turn in.' Alfred did not watch him to see if he did go in: it would be easy for Bert to escape. But he was thinking that if he were Betsy, he would watch, and intervene, if he had to.

It was very warm and a breath left dust on the tongue. The scent of the may was like a clammy touch.

Shadows from a long line of elms that stood along a stream stretched to his feet. A cart that had sacks of barley on it went past in the lane. The smell of the barley, sweet and insidious, made Alfred think of a tankard of ale, with a big head on it.

'Oh, Lord,' said Alfred. 'I'm catching Bert's condition.'

He had had a bad afternoon. First, he hated seeing his Betsy swollen and reddened, her hair matted on her cheeks. He was thinking all afternoon, trying to come to terms with it, that two years ago he had seen little Betsy, a delicately plump pretty girl, at the hospital dance, and he had swept her away from her partner in the Excuse Me, then danced with her all evening. And that had led to this, with him sitting here, perplexed and disbelieving, with one ear open for Bert – in the room at the corner of the house – his wife lying down because she felt bad, and him …

As he was coming away from the station, having left Betsy there with Bert in the train, two girls had called out to him, 'Alf, Alf, will we see you tonight at the Dawley dance?'

Mr Redway had looked sharply at Alfred, who was about to call back, 'Yes, of course you will,' but then he remembered and said, 'I'm a married man, you've forgotten.' The girls were Ruby and Ethel and he had danced with both at many dances. His mother would have said they were common, but he didn't mind that. After all, he wasn't marrying them! They were good fun and, above all, they danced well.

'So,' called Ruby, 'your dancing days are over, Alf.'

And Ethel, 'What a shame, Alfred.'

A knife in his heart could not have hurt more. Yes, his dancing days were over, and he did so love to dance. He had won prizes for it. Often when he was dancing the floor cleared so that he and his partner – Ruby perhaps? Ethel? – could show off what they did. But his dancing days were over. If he had not had a wife lying there behind drawn curtains he would be off walking to Dawley. To walk on this summer evening, the shadows deepening, the birds sending to him their goodnight messages. Oh, no, he could not bear it. Never again. And so Alfred sat on the bench as the elm shadows engulfed his feet, and then his legs. He had understood that, with a wife, he could no longer enjoy the freedoms of a bachelor but he had not taken it in as he had that afternoon with 'Your dancing days are over.'

He had made himself go up to see how the workmen were getting on with the house, so soon to be needed; he had walked from one end of the farm to the other and then back and around. His walking days were with him still but his dancing days ...

Not long before it was time to set out for the station with his father-in-law, it occurred to him: And how is *she* feeling? I hadn't thought of that.

At the wedding in Kent he had seen how many of the young men were regretful – they had courted Betsy, or thought they might. He felt like a thief snatching away the favourite of the girls. He could see she was that. He had danced at the wedding, proud as could be, with this girl, a beautiful little dancer, light as a feather. They whirled in the waltz, they were clapped by the wedding guests for their quickstep, he heard the women saying, 'What a dancer!'

But his dancing days were over.

And Betsy, with her great stomach that seemed to swell as you looked at it, what did she feel? He hated that stomach. He felt the great protuberance had swallowed up his Betsy, his dancing girl. *But how did she feel?* Perhaps she felt as he did. With the shadows heavy on the garden Alfred turned and stood looking at Bert's window. It would have been easy for Bert to go out the back way and no one would have known. As he looked, he saw Bert was lighting the lamp. The glow of lamplight fell into the evening shadows. Bert had seen him,

Alfred, looking, and had lit the lamp to say he was there. Spied on, watched, suspected … that was Bert's life now and must be – for how long? And Betsy, how did she feel about that? She had married handsome Alfred Tayler, and found she had a brother-in-law who was drinking himself to death, and there was the whiny, complaining mother-in-law. Very strange if Betsy was not making comparisons.

Alfred went in, and into the bedroom, hoping that Betsy was asleep. He brushed his teeth as quietly as he could but as he lowered himself down beside her, careful of that great stomach, her arms went around him and he felt the hot, sweaty, distressed bundle that was his lovely Betsy.

'Oh, Alfred,' she said, 'I was waiting for you.' Waiting, he knew, for reassurance. Did he not need it just as she did? Two people, their dancing years behind them. He could not stop the sour words crowding his tongue.

'I was lying here thinking,' said Betsy. 'It is only two years since we first met. Do you remember, Alfred?'

Did he remember!

'And look at us now, Betsy,' he murmured, stroking her shoulders under the bundle of damp fair hair.

'Are you sorry you married me, Alfred?' came the sad little cry in his ear.

'No, how could I be? But you could be sorry, it seems to me. You're landed with quite a load.' And he was thinking of Bert, the heaviness of him, the weight of him, the threat – and now it was falling to Betsy to keep that load steady.

'Don't be sorry, Alfred. Oh, don't be sorry,' she pleaded into his ear.

'It seems to me that there are two of us who could be sorry,' said Alfred, trying to avoid that hot, treacherous stomach, which he knew could seethe and heave as you looked at it.

And then, in a little dry humorous voice that matched his own ironies, she said, 'But it's no use either of us regretting it now.' And she took his hand and put it just there, on what he feared, that mound – his child. Oh, and how could anyone expect him to make sense of that?

'We're stuck with each other, Alf,' said Betsy, putting her hand over his where it lay on what seemed to him must be a hand or foot or a knee thrusting out – as you could see on the side of a cow, near her time.

'Yes, so we are,' said Alfred, and swallowing his regrets, reluctance, reservations, he laughed quietly and said, 'Betsy, I was going to say, "But we've got each other," but it seems to me we've got a good bit more than that.'

And laughing, near to tears, they drifted off to sleep.

Emily suddenly understood that she had not thought about anything but her house, or rather William's house, for months – years? Curtains, wallpapers, the cover for a chair, a new dining-table, carpets, rugs had filled her mind, day and night. All her concentration, her energy, had gone into it, as if for an examination. This realization had come to her when she was visiting Daisy, where she had not been for some time, being too busy with soft furnishing. She laid in front of Daisy swatches of silks, velvets, velveteen, and saw Daisy's face, which was saying, 'Well, then, what has got into you, Emily?' What had? Sitting in the little sitting-room at Daisy's, with Daisy and the woman who had taken her place in the house, one Dido, once her own staff nurse, now sister in the ward Sister McVeagh had ruled, it seemed as if she had been under a spell. The swatches of fabric now seemed like a comment on the absurdity of her, Sister McVeagh. This was not what she was.

Here, where she had lived with Daisy, gossiping about hospital matters, she felt she had never left the Royal Free. Her life since her splendid marriage was as if someone else had lived it.

Daisy shrewdly contemplated her friend, and remarked, 'Well, Emily, I would never have believed you could care about all this.' Daisy was still a little thing and, beside the well-fleshed Emily, seemed she might blow away or disappear if you stamped your foot.

Emily was thinking wildly that she would not leave here, it was where she belonged. Even Mrs Bruce, seeing her go up the stairs, seemed pleased. 'Welcome home,' she said as a joke, but it chimed with Emily's feeling.

Her husband, the eminent doctor, was going to a professional dinner tonight so Emily could stay … and she stayed. She pushed the pretty fabric away into her purse and talked about events at the Royal Free as if she had never left.

When she got home her William was getting ready for bed.

He had drunk a little too much – but God forbid this could be compared with Bert's excesses. He was in a good mood, and kissed Emily more warmly than usual. Feeling he appreciated her, even actually saw her, made her expand into recklessness, and as he put his arms around her, she said, 'Oh, what would you say if I went back to the Royal Free?' This shows she was not a tactful wife: surely the wrong time and place for such an impetuous announcement. He dropped his arms, stood staring at her while disapproval took him over. He said, 'That wouldn't be very nice for me, would it, Sister McVeagh?'

But when they were slowly coming to an understanding, Dr Martin-White and Sister McVeagh, hadn't it been very nice indeed? He turned away and got into his own bed: they had separate beds.

So that was that! No question of it.

And the way he had said *Sister McVeagh* told her that he had not entirely admired her, or did not now.

Well, he could hardly stop her, could he? Yes, he had, with one cold remark.

Emily, who had seen very little of Daisy, went there as much as she could. She felt so excluded, left out, *shut* out.

If the Emily who had thought, bought, shopped for, ordered, even dreamed of wallpapers and paints for so long – she was going to have to admit it was a good deal more than a year – if this Emily suddenly seemed alien to her, then Mrs Martin-White, the doctor's wife, seemed even more so. She was desperately unhappy, though at first she thought she was ill. What could account for her heavy heart, her anxiety, her feelings of wild panic that took her over for no reason, without warning? In those days people did not automatically search in their memories of childhood to explain current wrongs. Yes, she had felt like this before, she knew she had, but could not remember why or when. She reminded herself that she had lost her mother, aged three, and presumably she had been unhappy then. But this, what she was feeling now, pain her element, unhappiness the air she breathed? And whom could she tell? She did remark to Daisy, when Dido was not there, that she felt low and bad and unhappy, and did not know why.

Daisy had no experience of being married or even thinking much about marriage. Emily, it seemed to her, had walked away from her, and her experience of her, when she had taken off into a state of – it seemed to Daisy – unnatural and wild exultation, planning that amazing wedding. That had not been the Emily she knew or had ever known.

Daisy was working for final examinations, which would make her an examiner of nurses. Her concentration on a goal was as fine as Emily's, but not so near an edge of instability. Daisy and her old colleagues had remarked that Emily did not seem herself these days, and so had Mrs Lane, Daisy's mother.

Emily wept a good deal in private, concealed red eyes and a need to sigh deeply and long … but she could not conceal her state from the servants, all four of them, the housekeeper ('who has been with me since my mother died'), the housemaid, the maid-of-all-work, the cook. Emily was irritable and often unreasonable, and they left.

'You are not the only woman who cannot deal with her servants,' was what her loving husband said to her. 'Well, get some more.'

But Emily, like her husband's colleagues' wives, complained about the servant problem, which was fast becoming a major crisis for the middle and upper classes.

The plenitude and wealth of Edwardian England had not ended. This was a time of great prosperity – well, it was for the said classes. And the servants were deciding that to work in private houses with their restrictions and rules was not for them. Within a mile or so of Clarges Street there were a new glove factory ('French' gloves), a French milliner, an upholsterer whose other shop was in Paris, a luxurious chocolate shop, a department store whose five floors were crammed with fashion and frivolity. And the craze for everything Russian, Mir. That was where Emily's servants had gone. She advertised in newspapers, applied to agencies, but she had a single housemaid and a maid-of-all-work and no one to wait at table. She wrote to Mrs Lane asking if the country girls might like to come and work for her. There was accommodation – well, of a sort – but Mrs Lane wrote back to say that the girls these days didn't want to do housework.

Meanwhile Emily remained so low, so sad, that her husband, noticing it, prescribed a tonic. He remarked, too, that Emily seemed to be spending a lot of time with nurses at Chestnut Street. And he suggested that this wife or that wife of his colleagues would surely be more suitable company.

Mary Lane was not surprised. She had thought from the

start that when the glitter of that wedding had worn off, Emily would be needing advice. From the moment she had seen the photograph of Emily's fiancé, her heart had sunk. 'Yes, it did sink into my boots,' she had told Daisy, who had said that Emily was not the old Emily, but perhaps this doctor of hers would be right for her new state, which was all fashion and furniture.

Emily and Mrs Lane sat outside the little house in garden chairs, where the road that led to the station was visible.

Mrs Lane waited for Emily's revelations, and chatted. A plump fair woman appeared in the lane with a pram, in which were two infants.

'That's Betsy, you know, Alfred's wife,' said Mrs Lane, and called out.

'It's late for their lunch,' called back Betsy, but wheeled the pram, bought by Mr Redway – 'You deserve the best money can buy' – a little way up the path.

'They are lovely babes; they are twin boys,' said Mrs Lane, waving at the three. 'Betsy, do come soon and let me indulge myself.'

Mrs Lane, with the new twins down the lane, had hardly been able to tear herself away, but then Betsy had said that she felt she could manage now, and Mrs Lane restricted her visits.

Betsy wheeled the pram near to the two women lolling in their chairs.

The babes were certainly most delightful, and Mrs Lane fussed a bit with them until she remembered that Emily was there for her attention. Betsy went off, slowly, homewards.

'I haven't managed to get pregnant,' remarked Emily.

'Well, it hasn't been very long, has it?'

'It didn't take her very long,' said Emily.

'Do you mind? Are you worried?'

And now Emily did not know what to admit to first. She wanted to talk to her friend, tell her about the unhappiness that was dragging her down. Not having got pregnant was the least of it.

Mrs Lane had expected confidences about the marriage bed, not to put too fine a point on it. That diffident, sensitive, fine-drawn man – Emily needed something more, well, more like herself, strong and forthright.

But today Emily seemed neither. Compare this Emily with the girl who had come to announce her wedding, alive with success, with accomplishment; victorious was the word Mrs Lane used of that Emily. The cat that had swallowed the cream. But now? She was thinking that William didn't seem much of a man – certainly not one right for Emily – but she wasn't going to introduce the subject. Mind you, it is easy to be wrong about the quiet ones, she had reflected.

No marriage counsellors in those days, but if Mary Lane had been one surely she would have warned of incompatibility. She was, however, a wise woman, and must have noted often enough that Nature does not seem to care much about the happiness of her children when making matches.

Emily finally got around to saying that she was so unhappy she could die, and she didn't care if that sounded silly.

But she didn't say why. Mrs Lane waited for her to confide,

say anything that could be latched on to, but no. She would have liked to ask, 'Do you have fun in bed?' as Betsy and Alfred did – Betsy was not shy about confidences. But to use the word 'fun' of serious Dr Martin-White – no, one could not.

Emily began to weep. She cried and cried, sitting on the grass by this woman whom she had always said was her real mother, and she put her head in Mrs Lane's lap and went on sobbing while Mary stroked her head.

'Emily,' Mrs Lane attempted, 'have you kept up with your music?'

'No, I suppose not.'

'And you used to be so busy … Are you playing tennis?'

'No.'

'Would William not want you to do that?'

'No, he would like me to play tennis – with the right people.'

And so Mrs Lane got nowhere and Emily went off back to London.

She could not tell Mary Lane what was wrong because she didn't know.

Emily had been brought up by an authoritarian father, in a strict cold house where everything went along by rule and rote. From that she escaped to the hospital, with its hierarchies, its disciplines, its order. She had lived her entire life bounded by rules and regulations and discipline. And now – there was nothing, and she did not know what it was she missed. That had been the start of this present misery: she felt cast out on to a sea of possibility with no chart. And there was worse. Her husband was not a loving man and there was certainly no fun in bed. But she didn't know enough to realize what she missed.

When she yearned to be back at the Royal Free, Sister McVeagh, it was the order, the certainties, she wanted.

Emily felt she was in a deep black pit, with tall smooth sides. In training, she had 'done' neurasthenia, but that aspect of nursing had not interested her. Now she was sorry. If she could have put a name to the dark pit, she would have felt better. But one thing she did have to hold on to. She would have to get herself out of this place. No one else could. Who had rescued her from her overwhelming father? She had. Only she. No one else.

'I am going to have music evenings,' she said one night, into the dark. She had not known until this moment that she was going to say this.

She knew her husband was lifting himself on his elbow to stare at her.

She had not said, 'We shall have ...' No. 'I am going to have ...'

The formidable machine of that energy of hers was behind that I. It was rescuing her.

She waited for disapproval, but all that came was, 'But with no staff, surely a social evening is not possible?' He hadn't said no, hadn't sent towards her a deadly ray of the disapproval, which, she felt, had pushed her over into the pit.

'You'll see,' she said. 'In the first place, I'm going to keep the staff at two: a cook-housekeeper and a housemaid. And I am going to send out the washing to the Chinese laundry …'

'I really cannot be expected to involve myself with these domestic arrangements,' said he. But he was leaning on his elbow still, looking through the dimness of the bedroom towards her.

In the hospital, Sister McVeagh would return from a visit to the laundries with a gay 'A vision of hell.' Or 'Abandon hope all ye who enter here.' She had hated that laundry and here it was again in her own home, the boilers, the mangles, the washboard, the steam irons, the pile of coal in the corner.

'I need you to know,' said Emily. 'We must agree on it. It will be expensive, the laundry, but with only two wages to pay … and I plan to get in staff for special occasions.'

'I see you have already planned it all,' said he. Was he still leaning up on his elbow?

He was not a mean man. Her household allowance was generous, and so was her dress allowance: he liked her to be well dressed. But it was bitter, that moment when he handed her the money in its separate envelopes. She had earned her own living since she was eighteen, and perhaps of the by now many things that dismayed her about her marriage, it was that moment, that money, handed her with a smile, that dismayed her most. *But that was not the point.*

'We have to agree,' said Emily, and now she was insisting on the *we,* was she? 'If we are going to have musical evenings and entertain, then the bill for wages will be more.'

She heard him settle back into bed. And he wasn't angry a bit. No, he was pleased, she could feel it. A most improbable conclusion was forcing itself on her. All this time he had been wanting her to be a hostess. 'That is what he married me for,' Emily told herself, incredulous. Me, Sister McVeagh. Is that how he saw me? That's why he chose me? (She was not saying, 'He chose me because he loved me.' That conclusion did not impress itself.)

A hostess. Me? And yet she did have it all planned out, and as she talked into the dark, new decisions, already made by her, apparently, came to her tongue, as if she had previously sat down with a piece of paper and a pencil.

'I am sure you will do it well, Emily,' was her reward that night.

Is that what he had been waiting for all this time? Could he not have said?

Emily made the change with the staff, and did something else. She went around the new smart shops that were offering all kinds of domestic novelties, and bought the very newest, one of the earliest vacuum-cleaners – clumsy and heavy, but what a revelation. She bought a dozen 'labour-saving' appliances. She had a telephone installed on every floor – a house then might have just one.

The first musical evening was a great success. She played well, and he had a pleasant tenor; some of the other doctors turned out to be talented.

She embarked on a dinner party; he chose the guests.

She had some luncheon parties, for the wives of his colleagues.

During this time an invitation came from Alfred and Betsy Tayler to the christening of their twin boys. But the date clashed with a party she was giving. Daisy went, stayed the night with her mother, and told Mrs Lane that Emily had turned into a socialite: 'You'd never believe it, Mother.' Mrs Lane did believe it; she kept an eye on Emily's doings through the gossip columns, where Dr William Martin-White's and Mrs Martin-White's parties often featured.

'She's going in for the Honourable this and Lady that,' said Daisy. 'She invited me to a musical do and I was sitting next to our ambassador in Berlin.'

'You know, Daisy,' said Mrs Lane, after a heavy silence. 'I don't like it. I don't *see* her in that life. That's not really Emily.'

But Emily was playing this role as if she had never done anything else.

'You wanted a hostess,' she might silently tell her husband. 'Is that what you wanted? Well, here I am.'

When he went off to some dinner or a meeting, Emily was with Daisy in that house she felt was really her home. Other nurses came and went, but Daisy kept on the flat.

Emily felt she was escaping when she went to Daisy's. And there, too, she heard news of her husband, the eminent cardiologist. She might have found him disappointing as a husband, but it was like a seal of approval on her choice to hear how highly he was held in the hospital, in the medical world generally.

But she often thought that she would not be able to stand her life if she could not have slipped off sometimes to be with Daisy in her old home.

Many a widow, thinking that the funeral, if not the reading of the Will, would mark the end of all that could be expected from her in the way of public griefs has found that some problems are just beginning.

William died unexpectedly of a heart-attack, without warning, in the spring of 1924, and none of the letters of condolence from the many Martin-Whites hinted at trouble, until one arrived from Cedric, a nephew, son of William's elder sister.

Do you remember me, Aunt Emily? I helped carry Uncle William's coffin last Monday. From something I heard you say it occurred to me that you have no idea of the busy intrigues that have been going on about your house. Did you know the family covet it? I thought I should warn you.

After the funeral there had been a formal goodbye to the popular Dr William Martin-White at the Royal Free Hospital. And some of the family, in the medical profession themselves, attended; but Emily had invited all the Martin-Whites, some of whom she had hardly heard of, to the house for sherry and cake on a Sunday afternoon.

The folding doors of the first-floor reception room had

been leaved back and there revealed was the capacious and elegant room where Emily and William had had their concerts. The grand piano, usually prominent, was pushed out of the way; so were the harp and the music stands. There were vases of cheerful daffodils, Emily having rebelled against the white flowers that had emphasized the funeral. She wore black, but had a large white collar: the parlourmaid she had hired for the afternoon also wore black, and a frilly white apron. In fact the scene was more festive than funereal and Emily expected reproaches, which came at once from William's sister, Jessica, who was in unrelieved black.

'My dear Emily,' said Jessica, 'how well you do look.'

If Emily had shed tears, any traces were well hidden. She urged her guests to help themselves from the trays that stood about. Cedric, an immediately engaging young man, rather military in style – the current vogue – arrived late, winked solemnly at Emily, and looked pretty well, if not jolly, himself.

'Now that we are together,' said Jessica, well supplied with sherry and fruit cake, 'I hope that there will be an opportunity for a discussion.'

'Oh? What about?' enquired Emily, acknowledging Cedric's contribution with not a wink – she could not have gone so far – but a smile.

There were about thirty people in the room and some of them Emily had not seen since the wedding. She did not know who they all were.

'Well,' enquired Jessica, brushing crumbs from her black folds, 'shall I begin?'

'Please do,' said Emily. 'But I am mystified.

The air was electric with the results of the 'intrigues' Cedric had warned against.

'Some of us feel, dear Emily,' said Jessica, 'that you might perhaps think it right to live in a perhaps rather less grand style. This is surely too large a house for one person.'

'Really?' said Emily. 'I had not decided to move.'

'Now surely, Emily,' said Jessica, 'it must have occurred to you that William would have wished for you to live more modestly.'

'But we know what William would have wished,' said Emily, 'because there was a Will, and the house was left to me.'

This sharp riposte, which was giving Emily a good deal of pleasure, did not please Jessica. But some people were recognizing that Sister Emily McVeagh was in the room, with her famously sharp tongue.

'Did dear William not perhaps indicate his wishes to you? He must have had thoughts.'

Here Cedric coughed, to hide a laugh, and Jessica looked hard at him. 'Not everyone agrees with the majority,' she said. 'Cedric, for one, said he hoped you would not end your music parties.'

'How could William have indicated anything, since he did not know he was due for a heart-attack?' said Emily. 'I don't think such a degree of prescience could have been expected.'

Cedric coughed again.

'Well, Emily, it is right that you know our thoughts. Your situation has been discussed, and at the very least you should take some notice of our wishes.'

'I am more concerned with William's wishes,' said Emily. 'Not that I had any idea that you were so concerned about me. When I have thought it all out, I shall of course let you know what I propose to do. But I shall not be throwing myself on to a funeral pyre.'

Cedric laughed outright and some of the younger members did too.

'We told Aunt Jessica you weren't going to go quietly,' said Cedric.

'Cedric,' rebuked Jessica. 'That was uncalled-for.'

'All that money William left you,' said Cedric. 'That's the trouble, you see. Naturally they want to know what you are going to do with it.' There, he had said it.

'Cedric!' said the older aunts and uncles. 'This is too bad.'

'Cedric, you are taking no care for Emily in her time of grief.'

'Well, you are, so that should be enough,' said Cedric.

There was a good deal of money. Emily had had no idea at all of the extent of her William's little fortune. It was large enough to be called that. His father had been a stockbroker, had invested well, and the family had lived frugally. Until, that is, William married Emily and then she had made the house so elegant and, above all, so up-to-the-minute with her house-keeping devices.

'Some of us have been thinking,' said Cedric, still determined to annoy the older Martin-Whites, 'that this house would be perfect for a young couple. I shall be getting married

– but I am already well housed. There's young Raleigh: he's marrying a cousin, so it would be kept in the family.'

Emily was annoyed, but entertained, too. How glad she was that William had not much liked his family, if this was how they went on.

'I shall bear in mind,' said Emily, 'that Raleigh and – who?'

'Rose,' said Jessica, regaining command of the proceedings. 'Raleigh and Rose. I am sure Rose would appreciate your wonderful domestic arrangements.'

'I shall keep in mind that Raleigh and Rose want my house,' said Emily. 'Now, how about some more sherry, Jessica – Cedric, Tony ...'

'You see, Emily,' said some old buffer, whom she seemed to remember was an uncle Henry, 'all that money, I am sure William would hate to think of it being frittered away.'

'Well, I don't propose to do the house up again – redecorate. Nor do I need a new wardrobe. So rest assured, Uncle Henry.'

Surely they must have been heartened that her ideas of extravagance were so limited.

'You could give this house to Raleigh and Rose and live in theirs in the country,' said a cousin.

'Why should I live in the country when I never have?' said Emily. 'Believe me, when I have made decisions, if any, I shall let you know.'

And so ended the family pow-wow on Emily's future.

Emily was in fact badly shocked by William's death and not

only because it was unexpected. She had thought of him as young – well, not old, not even middle-aged. He had been fifty, surely not of an age when one thought of anything definite, like retirement, let alone death. But what was throwing her into a perplexity was that her life had become so bound up with his; since they had married everything she had done and thought had been for William. And where was Emily McVeagh? Not so far away, obviously. But for ten years that was what she had done: she had been William's. And now what? She was forty. She could go back to nursing if she wanted. Already suggestions had been coming her way. She felt torn loose, floating …

She could marry again. But she could not imagine a man she would want to marry. However one put it, she had been married to William for better or for worse. After ten years, what kind of profit or loss could be made? She did not know how to start. And if she could not say what had happened to her – and she saw it, felt it, as something, somebody, taking up the strands of her life and twisting them up with his – then how could she even begin to think what to do next? She had been Emily McVeagh, a decided, definite, bold character, and now she was nothing; she was something that drifted.

Daisy? But even thinking of her as something to grasp hold of, be with, as they once were, was barred now, because Daisy was doing so well, so solidly grounded in what she was and did that Emily felt she would be like a little probationer tugging at Daisy's skirts. And, besides, Daisy had hinted that she was thinking of marrying herself. There was this surgeon at the hospital, and it seemed Daisy 'would not mind' – her words. She was thinking of it – well, not immediately, of course, but they were not youngsters.

Emily had no one to hold fast to, no one even to consult. How could she talk about her state, after years of marriage, and such an encompassing marriage, with someone who said she 'would not mind' when thinking of a man to marry.

She had no one. No one. And no child, nothing.

But she had Mary Lane, and remembering her, it was like stumbling on a beam from a lighthouse.

She would shut up this house, and go down to stay with Mary Lane. This was impulsive, impetuous, a decision made between going to bed one night and getting up in the morning.

Of course, that was what she would do, must do.

Emily ran up the path to Mary Lane. It was supper-time, twenty-four hours after she had made her decision.

Her old friend stood at the stove, with a large pan. 'I'm cooking you pancakes,' she said, 'because you like them so.'

Emily dropped her case, flung herself into a chair at the old table, where Harold Lane already sat, and said, at Mary's diagnostic look, 'In every life some rain must fall.' She had been using this to ward off emotions, her own too, since the death, but now she burst into tears. She sat and sobbed.

'That's right,' said Mary. 'You have a good cry.'

'The poor woman has lost her man,' remarked Harold.

This almost stopped Emily crying, but the words were

fastened on by a disordered brain, and she thought, That's right. It's true. But she had not thought it before. The kindly remark, a simple message of the sort that always did relieve her of anxiety, was balm and solace, as if none had been offered her.

She glanced at Harold Lane, whom she had not noticed much before, he being so dependent on Mary, and thought, Funny he should say something so right when I need it.

Mary put pancakes and lemon on Emily's plate, and some more on her husband's, and sat down.

Emily began staunching tears and trying to smile. She felt as sick and as sorry as she had ever done in her life. But here she was, where she so needed to be, with Mary, and she looked about her and felt as if this was a dream, where familiar things had undergone change. This was the old kitchen she had sat in so often, and here were Harold and Mary. Everything seemed so dim, so muted, and it was not because she looked through tears. She had come here from her bright, light, clean house, and it seemed that there was dust on what she looked at, or a dimness. The big room was all dull pinks and browns, and even the cat on the arm of a chair seemed dingy. She remembered a white cat.

And Harold and Mary ... how long was it since she was here? Months, surely, yes, more, many months, years ... The two had grown large. They were ample, red-cheeked people with their fair strawy hair going grey.

'I daren't eat anything these days,' mused Mary. 'I am getting so fat.'

'Nonsense,' said Harold. 'The more the merrier.'

And now Emily began to laugh. It was strained, and hysterical, but better than crying.

Emily sat there in her sharp London black and made the kitchen even dingier.

'You'd better leave off that mourning,' said Mary. 'No one will expect it of you here.'

Emily said, 'I don't think I've got anything to wear.' Her case was full of smart clothes.

'And don't you fret,' said Mary. 'So, it's turned out lucky I've gained weight. I'll find something for you after supper.'

Harold said he was going to read his papers in his lair; Emily helped Mary wash up, and then Mary came from her room with armfuls of clothes, and some of them Emily thought she did remember.

Emily slipped off her short black skirt, put on a longer brown one, dreadfully out of fashion, and a yellowish blouse. She looked pretty good, even then.

'What a talent you have,' sighed Mary. 'You could always make a smart show out of any old skirt and blouse.'

She lit the lamp and sat opposite Emily.

'I feel so bad, Mary. I don't know what to do with myself.'

'But did you expect to feel anything else?'

'I don't know what I expected.'

The cat jumped from her armchair to Mary's lap.

'If I had a child ... but it never happened.'

Mary stroked the cat, which purred steadily.

Emily watched that large, strong hand. 'What am I fit for

now, Mary? I didn't think like that when I was doing it, but for ten years now all I've done is lunches and dinners and suppers, and looked after William.'

'If I were you I shouldn't think at all about it,' said Mary. 'Just let yourself have a bit of a rest.'

'A rest?' said Emily. 'I don't think I've rested in my life.'

'Well, then,' said Mary. Soon, she dislodged the cat, handing it to Emily, and brought out a big cardboard box full of coloured papers.

'I have a new occupation,' she said. 'There's a child here most days. I don't know if you ever noticed Bert? His wife, Phyllis, is having her second and I'm looking after their first for a little.'

This was what had happened.

Betsy harried and chivvied Bert until he promised to give up the drink for good.

'It's the only way,' said she. 'And didn't the doctor tell you the same?'

Bert stopped drinking, or nearly, until there was a bad night when he fell down and was concussed.

'And now that's it, Bert,' said Betsy.

Alfred did help, as well as he could, but it was Betsy who cured Bert.

Two years passed and then there was this conversation. It was in Alfred and Betsy's sitting-room, in their new house.

'Bert, who is this girl you go about with?'

She knew, of course.

'That is Phyllis Merton and she wants to marry me.'

'Yes, but do you want to marry her, Bert?'

'Now that is the question. You know who I want to marry. I want to marry you.'

'Oh, Bert, you are so silly sometimes.'

Bert, sober, had kept some of his bumbling, foolish-old-dog ways, partly because he was rather like that, but also because when he was drinking it had been hard always to tell when he was drunk and when not.

Did that mean he planned to return to drink one of these days? Betsy did wonder, and then asked him. 'Bert, you put on all these foolish ways, and they are funny. I'm not saying they aren't, but sometimes I wonder if you are serious about never drinking again.'

'Clever Betsy. Sometimes I wonder myself. To give up for ever – have you thought of that? Longer than a lifetime.'

'But when you marry, Bert, you mustn't ever drink, not ever.'

'That's the trouble, you see, Betsy.'

'Do you like her, Bert?'

'But do you like her? I'd never marry a girl you didn't approve of.'

'I hope she is a real little termagant, like me,' said Betsy.

That was what Alfred sometimes called her.

'Well, then, Alfred. Have I stopped him drinking or haven't I?

'Because you see, Bert, being married, sometimes things are quite difficult. And you'll be tempted to start off again.'

'I'll marry her if you approve,' said Bert.

Phyllis was a farmer's daughter from Ipswich way, and she had been thoroughly looked over by everyone concerned. It was generally agreed that she was after not just Bert, a nice enough chap now he was sober, but the Redway farm. Now, that was not something to be turned down.

On the whole people approved. She was a thin, dark, clever girl, always on the watch, observing, noticing. It was these last qualities that Betsy approved.

'She'll be good for you, Bert. She'll keep you on the straight. And I must say I'll be so pleased to have her take over. You've sometimes worn me out, Bert. Many a time I've gone to bed crying because of you, worrying so much over you.'

'Then to please you I'll marry Phyllis,' said Bert, in his foolish-old-dog mode.

The Redways approved. Rather, Mr Redway did. Mrs Redway did not find much in life to agree with her these days. There was a big wedding. Betsy was matron of honour. There were bridesmaids, ten of them, and the little church at Long-erfield was full. Alfred's father played the organ.

Alfred was best man.

It went on well enough until Phyllis got pregnant, and there were difficulties. Bert came often to Betsy for counsel and advice.

The baby, a girl, was born, was healthy, but Bert had a relapse. Phyllis being busy with the baby, Betsy dealt with the relapse. 'Never again, Bert. You promised, didn't you?'

After quite a time Phyllis got pregnant again and it was then Mary Lane had stepped in to help with the little girl.

Phyllis had a mother, but she didn't live only a short lane away, like Mary.

Mary adored the little girl, who adored her.

'It looks to me as if this is as near as I'll get to being a grandmother,' she mourned, 'so I shall make the most of it.'

Emily woke not knowing where she was or, indeed, who she was. Then, the lowing of cattle, not too far away, told her that this was not London. It was very quiet. Warm pressure on her legs absorbed her attention. It was the cat. Emily shifted her knees, and the cat woke and yawned.

What Emily needed, she now knew, was to find Mary, and to hear from her words that would define her, her situation.

She went to the kitchen in her wrap, and saw that any breakfast had been eaten long ago. It was already mid-morning. Emily found water simmering in the kettle, made herself tea, and sat down. She decided she must be ill. She could not remember being ill. Her heart ached, but if that was a symptom, then … There were voices, one a child's from outside. A window from the kitchen showed the two, Mary Lane and a little girl, engrossed in each other, in a small room like a conservatory that had windows on to a garden.

The sight of Mary, bending forward to smile at the child, who was cutting out coloured paper with blunt scissors, made Emily's heart go cold with misery. The child leaped on to Mary's capacious knees, and Mary hugged and kissed Josie, Bert and Phyllis's child. Still Emily did not realize that what she wanted was to be that child, rocked in Mary's arms.

Emily retreated to the table, and her tea, and stayed there, listening to the sounds of woman and child, from time to time going to the window to see how it all went on. What total absorption from Mary. If she, Emily, had had a child, was that how she would have been? In the ten or so years she had been a dedicated hostess, could she have spent her time as Mary was now?

There would have been something to show for it, whereas now she kept thinking: But that wasn't me, surely. Was it really me in that nice house that took up so much of my attention?

At lunch-time Mary brought in the child, for some little mess or other, and Emily was offered plates of this and that. Mary hardly ate. 'She will have a nap now,' she said. 'Well, a small child certainly does tell you your limitations.'

The child went with Mary to her bedroom, and Emily, glancing in, saw that both were asleep.

She went out into the lane, which had not changed, and she wandered along past clumps of daffodils and narcissi till she saw a big field, which she remembered. But it was full of noisy children running about, and then she saw a man she associated with cricket. Yes, that was Alfred Tayler and he was instructing what seemed like hundreds of children of various sizes, boys and girls, in the ways of cricket. Emily sat down, where she had before, under the oaks, to watch. It was all very noisy and energetic and when the cricket ball arrived near her feet, a much earlier Emily jumped up and threw the ball back towards the man, who caught it, with a laugh and little bow.

Soon he came over, and said, 'I am sure I know you. But I am confused. That skirt ...'

'I am wearing Mary Lane's clothes,' said Emily. 'I came down on an impulse and didn't bring the right things.'

'Oh, yes,' said Alfred. 'I see. I heard from Mary that you've had bad luck.'

Well, that was a way of putting it.

'Yes, my husband died.'

'That is very sad. I'm sorry.'

'I've seen you playing cricket before, long ago.'

'Not so long, surely,' said Alfred, gallantly, as two boys came running up. 'These are Tom and Michael,' said Alfred. The two loud, excited boys were tugging their father away, back to the cricket pitch.

Alfred ran, the boys chasing him.

Could I have done that? wondered Emily. The boys were likeable lads, both dark and lean: like their father, she supposed.

She sat on, watching until Alfred came running back to say that tomorrow, if she liked, he would be doing sports with the children over there. There, she could see, were two workmen pushing a heavy roller each.

Alfred went running off, surrounded by the children.

The cottages and houses of the Redway farm were full of children. Emily went back to the Lanes' to find a heavily pregnant woman taking the child by the hand to lead her away from Mary.

'No, it does me good to walk,' she said, though she was scarlet and perspiring and full of discomfort, Emily could see.

A dark woman, but it was not possible to see what she would look like when not pregnant.

'I'm glad it's not long to go for her,' said Mary. 'Being in the family way isn't poor Phyllis's line at all.'

And now, until supper-time, Mary told Emily about how 'everyone' was concerned that any troubles Phyllis might have would start Bert off drinking again. 'That is the problem, you see.'

What interested Emily was the 'everyone'. And when Harold came back from the bank he too joined in, with how Alfred's wife was wonderful with Bert, no one knew what could have happened if Betsy hadn't been so good with Bert, because there was a time when everyone thought he was going straight towards the DTs.

Again Harold went off to the room he called his lair, and Mary said she was at her wit's end, there were mice again in the storeroom and really she thought that Mrs Mew – the cat – wasn't earning her keep.

This house had been a farmhouse once, before it was absorbed by others, which collectively now wanted to be called a village. At the back there was a pantry, with marble shelves, where stood bowls of cream and milk, cheeses, ranks of eggs, slabs of yellow butter. Off that was the storeroom, with sacks of oats, flour, sugar, and on the floor piles of potatoes and onions, covered from the light.

Here, Mary mourned, a family of mice left their droppings on the floor and even in the pantry.

The provisions of the storeroom, the pantry, were attractive to Emily, contrasting them with the tight, orderly shelves in her house in London where food arrived, delivered every day.

Mary said, 'Oh, Emily, I'm sorry. I'm off to bed. I know you must be feeling neglected.'

'It's enough to be here,' said Emily, thinking that with Mary just there, a yard or so away, it was indeed enough. But she would have liked very much to go with Mary to the kitchen for a good old-fashioned unhurried chat.

'You're not one to be knocked off course so easily,' said Mary, after a close look at Emily's forlorn face. 'You're all right.' And she went off to bed.

With that Emily had to be satisfied, but she lingered a while in the storeroom. Mrs Mew wandered in, like a visitor, just as if she did not know more was expected of her, and sat staring indifferently at a little hole in the corner, which Emily supposed must be a mousehole.

She drank cocoa. Now, when had she last done that? Yes, it was at Daisy's: they had been drinking cocoa last thing at night all through their training, and when Emily went to visit her.

Emily went to bed and thought that she had been here not two full days and was already feeling promptings of remorse about her listless state. She was not one to be knocked off course, had said Mary. Well, she had been, knocked down, knocked to pieces. And what *was* her course?

The next day the little girl came again to be with Mary, and Emily went off in the afternoon to watch the children with two men, one the energetic, always-on-the-move Alfred, and a tall, lazy, shambling fellow she supposed was the famous Bert. She sat away a little distance, hiding from the chilly spring airs in Mary's fur coat, which she suspected was rabbit, nothing like the sleek black moleskin of her own town coat.

There would be a big sports day tomorrow for the children of the area, and Emily planned to be there, but next day Phyllis called for Mary, saying she felt some pains but did not know if these were real birth pains but please would kind Mary …

Emily was left with Josie in the little conservatory, or semi-outdoors room. Josie showed she was well used to liking all kinds of different adults by liking Emily, at once climbing on her lap and expecting to be rocked and held.

Emily was thinking, amazed, But I've done all this, it's not true that I am useless at it. Of course, she had loved doing her stint during training in the children's wards. Sister Emily McVeagh had loved children – so it had gone – and Josie was being held in practised arms.

But then there was the day ahead, and Emily had to entertain the child, who expected it.

The cat wandered in. Josie knew and liked it. The cat wandered out.

'Where is she going?' asked Josie, and this casual enquiry began it all: everything in Emily's new life began just then.

'I think she is going to the storeroom. There are mice there.'

'Yes, pussies love mice,' mused this country child. 'Poor mice. Well, I hope she doesn't find them.'

'I think these mice must be clever. They have been living in the storeroom for some time.'

'But the cat is bigger than they are.'

'But they are clever,' said Emily. 'They hide when she chases them.'

'I wonder where they hide?'

'Mr Lane leaves his outdoor boots in the storeroom. I expect they hide in those.'

'Yes, and the cat can't get into the boots, can she?'

'No, the mice creep right down into the toes and wait until the cat goes off and they can creep out.'

'I wonder what the mice like to eat best?'

'I think, cats.'

'And cheese,' said the child. 'I like cheese.'

'Let's look and see.' And Emily and Josie went to the storeroom. On the way the child picked up Mrs Mew, who remained limp until they reached there, when she energetically twisted free and ran off back to her chair.

Emily and Josie surveyed the plenty of the pantry. The eggs rose up a wall on their racks, and Josie said, 'I think a mouse would like to eat the eggs, but how would it get through the shells?'

'A clever mouse would push an egg off and it would crash on the floor and then all the mice could gather around and eat it.'

'Look, there are Mr Lane's boots. If the egg fell into a boot

I expect Mr Lane would be cross with the mice.'

'Or suppose Mr Lane put on a boot and found something wriggling down at the end, and he said, Who is that nibbling at my toe?'

Josie found this hilarious and flung herself on to the floor to laugh.

Back in the little room where her toys were, she ignored them and said, 'Tell me some more about the mice.'

And then began the epic tales of the mice, their adventures with the stores, the eggs, the cheese, the cat … Emily had had no idea she could do this, keep up the invention of storytelling as long as the child said, 'And then? What happened then?'

Mary Lane came back, said that Phyllis was probably going into labour but the midwife was coming. She heard some of Emily's inventions and, like the child, said, 'Do go on, Emily.'

And Emily went on.

Next morning, a little friend of Josie's came with her to spend the day with Mary Lane and both at once clamoured for 'A story – tell us about the mice.'

The children could not get enough of the mice and their adventures, of Mrs Mew and hers, and then there were the birds in the branches, visible through the windows on to the garden.

'More!' chanted the children.

Mary sat in a rocking-chair in a corner and smiled, and said again, 'Emily, you are so good at it. Where do you get all these ideas from?'

'I don't know,' said Emily.

More children came. They crowded into the little room and Mary provided milk and cake and apples.

Then some bigger children arrived, among them Alfred's boys, but would they be satisfied with the adventures and ordeals of mice and blackbirds?

Emily widened her repertoire to include the many dogs of the farm, as well as the cats, the rabbits that could often be observed from these very windows. She found herself enquiring from Harold and Mary about the habits of ferrets, foxes and badgers. Then a message came from Mr Redway, brought by the boys, that he would be obliged if she could go there and confirm that Tom really did have some musical talent, which was what his teacher had said.

Along went Emily through the fields, and found Mr Redway, Mrs Redway, Alfred, a pretty fat woman, who was Betsy, and the two boys.

There was a good grand piano in the Redways' sitting-room: all the farmhouses and cottages had uprights. The children sang easily and without shyness, and snatches of music were part of the storytelling.

Tom stood by the piano as she played, watched by the family, and Emily put him through his paces, said, 'Yes, your teacher is right. He should have music lessons.'

'That can be arranged,' said Mr Redway at once.

'I don't know where he gets it from,' said Betsy. 'Not from me.'

'It's my father,' said Alfred. 'The child's grandfather. I think he has spent his life in that church, playing the organ.'

Messages were coming to the Lanes for Emily, from all kinds of parents, asking her to come and judge their off-spring's talents.

Meanwhile, the storytelling was going on, and every day there were more children.

'They are hungry for it,' said Emily.

'Starving for it,' said Mary. 'And, so, what are you going to do, Emily?'

At this point Daisy came down to visit her parents, partly because Emily was there. She arrived at supper-time and the four went to the table.

Mary had been cooking all morning. 'Daisy does like a nice bit of stew.' 'She loves rice pudding, if it has some nutmeg.' Daisy's appetite had always been something for any mother to despair over, but Mary seemed to have forgotten that, and Emily held her peace.

Daisy's weekend case was smart and new and so was her jacket, and Emily thought, That's for the benefit of Rupert, then. Daisy didn't much care about smartness. Rupert was Daisy's fiancé, and almost before they sat down Harold said, 'And when are we going to have the honour of meeting this chap of yours?'

Mary had met Rupert at a lunch in London, but Harold had only been told. 'He's very nice,' Mary had reported, but there was a tone in her voice that meant more could have been said.

'I thought of bringing him down for a weekend soon,' said

Daisy, and Emily knew Daisy was carefully not saying how very busy her distinguished surgeon was.

Mary did go up to London to see Daisy and there had been shopping trips, and she had seen where Daisy worked, watched the life of the busy hospital, but she did not know what Daisy did, thought, or how she spent time off. Her experience had been so far from her daughter's yet she longed to know more. Her over-timid questions to Daisy were meant to provide information she could understand, even start discussion. Daisy did not like this probing and replied briefly.

The table was laden with hardly touched dishes, though Harold took second helpings, mostly to please Mary.

'And I expect you girls will want to have your talk,' said Mary, and got up to light the candles on the sideboard. She was prepared to concede the usefulness of electric light, but she preferred lamplight and candles.

When Emily and Daisy went into the room Emily had been using, Daisy lit a candle beside her bed and Emily lit hers.

Daisy put on a nightdress with sleeves and a high neck, but Emily had pyjamas of dark blue, with scarlet piping. They sat up in bed and brushed their hair. Daisy had kept her coil of already greying fair hair, and Emily had a shingle. She had been saying to Mary that a shingle needed cutting once a week and she thought she'd give it up. The shingle and the bobs Emily's smart friends wore had begun because of the riots and civil wars that marked the end of the Hapsburgs. The insurgents and rebels wore very short hair. Turkey, falling into the same chaos of rebellion, provided the fashionable world with coiffures supposed to be modelled on what people imagined of the seraglio.

Both women vigorously brushed while the candle flames swayed.

Then Daisy remarked, 'Mary wrote and told me that you have all the children of the district hanging on your words.'

Emily let her brush drop and said, 'Oh dear. Oh, Daisy, what have I done?' And she burst into tears, and flung herself back on her pillows.

Daisy let her brush rest and said, 'But, Emily, whatever is the matter?'

'Have I done wrong? Did she complain? Oh, Daisy ...' And the sobbing intensified.

Daisy sat up straight, and said, 'Emily!' in a scandalized voice. 'What has got into you, Emily? Stop it at once.'

Emily muffled her sobs. 'All these children coming here and Mary feeding them and being so kind.'

'But, of course, she loves it.'

'I didn't know it would happen, Daisy. It just – happened.'

'But, Emily, it's wonderful. *Stop it.*'

'Is it? Is it?'

'Everyone admires you for it. You never did things by halves, did you? Stop crying.'

It was occurring to Daisy that Emily had recently lost a husband, but Daisy had secretly believed her friend would be pleased to get rid of him. William, as a poetical young doctor, had had all the nurses in love with him. But William Martin-

White was a different matter, stiff and severe, and people were afraid of him. She was. It did not occur to her that she herself was a pretty formidable figure in the hospital hierarchy.

Daisy enquired, 'Are you thinking of marrying again, Emily?'

'God, no,' said Emily, forcefully.

This confirmed what Daisy had thought and now she said, 'Put out your candle. I want to tell you something.'

Emily obeyed. It was a little blue enamel candlestick, and the candle was a stump. She loved the pretty candlestick, and often left the candle burning, as a sort of company.

'Now, Emily,' said Daisy, lying down, but leaving her candle burning enough to see if Emily had become herself again, 'I haven't told you this, I am pretty sure, I've been running around and around, because of Rupert. He wants a wedding soon … But, you see, he is involved with a society for the children of the East End. I am sure you know this, but there is such dreadful poverty there.'

Emily had not for years been conscious of much poverty. The people who had come to her parties were all well-off, if not rich. When she came to think of it, servants were the closest she had come to London poverty. Here, in the weeks she had been with the Lanes, she had visited the Redways in their fine house and had not been in the cottages of the farm workers. Their children, she thought, were not lacking in anything. They were warmly dressed and had plenty to eat. She believed their schools weren't up to much, though.

Britain was wealthy, was booming, was at a level of

prosperity the leader writers and public figures congratulated themselves and everybody on. Britain had not had a war since the Boer War; nor were there wars in Western Europe, which was on a high level of well-being. It was enough only to contrast the dreadful situation of the old Austrian Empire and the Turkish Empire, in collapse, to know that keeping out of war was a recipe for prosperity.

Various skirmishes in Africa, which could have grown worse, were damped down, because 'Why spoil what we have?' France, Germany, the Low Countries were booming.

But the riches of Britain, which was as full of big houses and high-living people as it in had been Edwardian times, did not seem to percolate downwards.

Daisy, keeping an eye on Emily in case she would start her crying again, sat up, and told her that the children of the East End ('and I'm only talking about London, mind you') were as pitifully ill-fed, unclad, dirty 'as a lot of little savages, Emily. Anyway, Rupert is going to set up this society, and we have a good many well-known supporters. We aim to change the East End. It is a disgrace that a great rich city like London should tolerate such poverty.' She went on for a while, saw that Emily had gone to sleep, and went to sleep herself.

Next day, Emily said she had taken in what Daisy had told her, and now that she was herself again, please would Daisy repeat it. While Emily and Mary admitted the hordes of children, 'Tell us a story, Auntie, tell us a story,' Daisy briefed Emily, and begged for her support. 'You are so good at this kind of thing, Emily. We need your energy, your efficiency. I've told Rupert you must be with us, and he says he remembers you very well from your time at the hospital. So all you have to do is to say yes.'

Emily said yes, but meanwhile other plans were hatching, which she discussed with Mary, who remarked that she wondered where Emily had got all her knowledge about books and stories. This caused Emily to write to her stepmother and ask if she could come and see her old books, if they still existed.

'Your room hasn't been touched, and your father, I am sure, would like to see you.'

Emily went to London, feeling she was leaving her true self behind. Perhaps she should find a farmer to marry, she mused.

The house in Blackheath had not changed, with not so much as a lick of paint. She refused to remember childhood scenes and feelings and went straight in to her father, who was, these days, very large and red-faced.

'You have had a loss, I hear,' said he. She had sent him a letter about her husband's death. 'He had a heart-attack, did he? I had a bit of a stroke myself.'

'Yes, it was a bad heart-attack.'

'I am careful what I eat and drink.'

She discussed her father's health for a while and then went up to her room, which her stepmother said had not been touched.

She found it the same as when she had left it twenty-two

years ago. She briefly swung open the door of the wardrobe, caught a glimpse of her schoolgirl clothing, and shut the door hard. She was furious.

There was an old oak bookcase under the window, and she sat in front of it, on the floor, and looked hard at the faded old books. First, there was a pile of maps, and atlases: yes, she had done well at geography. On what principle had these books been chosen? Books had just appeared, addressed to her, and she had taken them to her room. *The Moonstone, The Woman in White.* Sherlock Holmes. *Peter Pan*: yes, indeed, she had wept over Peter Pan. George Meredith, all of Dickens, from the look of it. All of Trollope. *Middlemarch* and *The Mill on the Floss.* William Blake: yes, she had had to recite 'O Rose, thou art sick' in class, but had had no idea what it was she was saying. The poems of Byron, Matthew Arnold, Shelley, Words-worth, Tennyson. Thomas Hardy – but not *Jude the Obscure. Moby Dick*, Hawthorne, John Keats. Shakespeare. The Lambs' *Tales from Shakespeare.* Lamb's essays. *Plain Tales from the Hills.* Palgrave's *Golden Treasury.* John Ruskin's *The Stones of Venice, Vanity Fair* … She had read lying on her bed, read here, where she was sitting. Books – a place of peace and calm, where she had been able to hide away from … Books were good. Reading was good. 'Are you going up to read, Emily? That's good.'

He had done well for her, her father. And on a table, piled tidily, copies of Walter Scott, in dark red leather bindings, but no one had read them. That was odd, wasn't it? She went down to say to her father, 'Thank you. You have no idea how well it has served me – reading.' But he was asleep and snoring. She found her stepmother and suggested that surely it was time to get rid of her girlhood clothes.

So, with the chill of that ancient rupture from her father still on her, she left, while at the same time blessing him: Thank you.

She visited several bookshops, said she would be ordering a lot of books, and enquired about trade prices.

She went back to the Lanes', triumphant.

'Thank you, Mary. It wouldn't have occurred to me to go and see what books I had,' and, when supper was over, she told Mary and Harold her plans, watching their faces for signs of doubt or disapproval. But both were pleased.

Harold said, 'I knew you wouldn't just mope about. It isn't in you.'

Mary said, 'I knew you'd come up with something really good.'

Harold went off to his lair, and the two women talked, until Mary said that Emily would need a good lawyer.

During this talk it emerged that Daisy would be in on these schemes. Not a word had been said by Daisy to her mother, nothing about her future, only that she wanted a quiet wedding, in a registry office, but if she, Mary, insisted, they could have a reception in a hotel – a small one.

Emily ended her news, saying, 'You've been so good to me, Mary. A girl doesn't need a mother if she has a friend like you.'

The two wept in each other's arms, but for very different reasons.

*   *   *

Emily wrote to Cedric Martin-White, and the two met in Emily's house, which she entered reluctantly. What a pleasant, bright, airy place it was, how much nicer and brighter than the Lanes' house, yet she felt it like a shadow enclosing her. It disapproved of her! Why? Oh, how fanciful and silly.

Cedric and Emily sat at the great table that had held so many of William and Emily's dinner parties. Cedric, told he would have to take notes, had brought notebooks and pencils and sat there, opposite Emily, the very essence of a responsible businessman. He was, in fact, a lawyer.

Having so recently expounded her plans to Mary, Emily had them at her fingertips and it did not take long to tell Cedric what she wanted.

He said at once that it did not seem clear what Daisy's and her Rupert's role was in all this. Were they discussing one or different organizations?

'I think we want roughly the same things.'

'I can make provisions for a society with similar parallel aims, or two societies. You are very sure of what you want, Aunt Emily.'

'Yes, very.'

'Then, why don't you set up a society or trust, or whatever we decide, run entirely by yourself? There is a great deal to be said for a single controlling voice. The more people you add, the more possible disagreements, and even quarrels. Do you know this Rupert?'

'Everyone knows of him. Rupert Fenn-Richards.'

'Oh, him. You should have said so. Because you'll need a list of people like bishops and the eminent to add respectability and renown to your proceedings.'

'Oh dear.'

'But if you are going to run this thing alone, I want to suggest you have me in. You can always twist me around your little finger, Aunt Emily. I am not likely to oppose your wishes. I like everything you say about it. A lawyer is always a good thing to have, you know.'

'Ideally, I'd like myself, Daisy Lane and you, then.'

'Would her husband be happy to be sponsor, to add a general sheen of honour? If he could rope in some more of his kind, so much the better.'

Emily said, 'And, after all, *I* know quite a lot of people of that kind.' So her dinner parties were turning out to be useful. 'As for Rupert, he's so busy I doubt he'd do much in the way of actual work. For that matter, if Daisy's going to be married, I expect the pressure will come on for her to stop.' Emily had no idea how resentful she sounded.

Cedric laughed and said, 'That emboldens me to make a further suggestion. That my fiancée, Fiona, come in with you as an active member.'

'But I've never met her,' said Emily, already jealous of ceding authority.

'But I hope that will soon be remedied. I hope you will agree to have lunch with us – perhaps tomorrow? She's mad keen on this idea of yours. What little you said in your letter was enough to fire her; she hasn't talked of anything else. She has already done a good bit of charity work in the East End, but nothing as good as your idea.'

'Suppose I don't like her?'

'Then say no. But I'll be able to wind her around my little finger. You'll see.' His smile was appropriate for a soon-to-be-married man, and Emily saw it and laughed.

'Oh, that is what you think now.'

'I don't want a wife who sits at home and has tea parties.' Then, seeing Emily was annoyed, he added, 'Of course, if she came up with anything as remarkable as your musical evenings ... Did I say she is a musician? She is. You really can't do everything yourself, Aunt Emily.'

Emily had in fact been visualizing just that, even though her secret musings included, We'll have our schools in all the cities of Britain.

'Tomorrow, lunch?'

'I am going to stay in a hotel,' said Emily. 'This place is giving me the creeps.'

'Do you think William has taken to a bit of haunting? I for one wouldn't put it past him. And for me, as you know I'll take this house off you within a week, if you like. Fiona would love it. Did I tell you she's a Lady in her own right?'

Emily looked across the traffic at a pavement where it seemed Cedric and his Fiona were in altercation. But they were laughing. They were surrounded by mostly young people, all gesticulating – jeering? – and laughing. It was like a chorus for a musical, with Cedric and Fiona as principals. Or was it a hairdressers' convention? She approached, dodging cars, seeing that every girl's head was in one of two modes. Some cheeks had on them a lacquered lock, like the 'cowlicks' of other times, looking like wood, so solid and sharp were they, in brown, yellow, black, blonde and even, once or twice, grey. The other coiffure was the one Emily already knew, the bunch of ringlets on each cheek, which meant a supporter of the Turks. As Emily arrived at the two, Cedric had his arm around Fiona, confronting an opposing crowd of ringleted girls. 'We are going to eat,' said Cedric. 'The food is good.' The ringleted girls gave way as Fiona went through them into the Turkish Delights restaurant. Her hair was in the other mode.

'I shall not introduce you,' said Cedric, embracing Emily too. 'By now you must be quite sick of hearing about each other.'

The proprietor, who knew Cedric, waved them to a table and pretended to tut-tut at Fiona's cheeks.

'Now, just show you are a free spirit,' said Cedric to Fiona, who might be laughing, but she was not far from tears. 'Rise above it.'

'It seems I have no alternative,' said Fiona, and pretended to shake her fist at some people pointing at her I-am-for-Serbia hairdo.

'Champagne,' said Cedric, which at once was brought. It seemed everyone was drinking champagne. In Longerfield people drank champagne on birthdays and special occasions.

'Aunt Emily,' said Fiona, 'I am so ashamed. How can you ever take me seriously after this?'

'I thought Aunt Emily would like to see how the death of empires can be celebrated by the way people do their hair,' said Cedric. 'Would you believe it, Aunt Emily? Last night here, just outside these two restaurants, this one, Turkish Delights, and the Last Word, next door, they were fighting because girls wearing ringlets went into the Serbs.'

'I wonder what the Serbs would say, or the Turks?' remarked Emily.

'Oh, how frivolous, yes, you are right. But don't forget, we are the surplus generation; we have to assert ourselves.'

A newspaper had come out with a leader saying the young men were restless because there had been no war, and they felt they had not been tested. 'They had been surplus to requirements.' At once the young men were wearing badges and buttons claiming they were Surplus.

Fiona, drinking champagne as if it were medicine, burst out with, 'Aunt Emily – I hope I may call you aunt. I am not a Martin-White yet, though I shall soon be … This has been such an unlucky start. I did so want you to take me seriously.'

'Of course she must take you seriously. She has seen you defy the opposing hordes of ringlet-wearers.'

'Aunt Emily,' insisted Fiona, 'I simply do have to tell you how much I admire this idea of yours.' And holding her champagne high so she could take restoring sips, she dabbed her wet eyes and, with scarlet cheeks, insisted, 'You see, I've been working in the East End now for months, and it is so awful. People never believe it when I tell them. The poverty is so bad. When I see the children, so thin, their poor little ribs sticking out, I simply can't believe that in this rich country of ours ...'

Clearly Fiona had already had some practice in public speaking, and Emily interrupted to say, 'But I was working with the poorest of the poor myself, when I was at the Royal Free.'

But Fiona was sweeping on. 'If I can do anything at all to help you, I will. When Cedric told me about your plans, it was my wildest dream come true.'

And so she went on, while the waiters brought their plates.

'Fiona,' said Cedric, 'just let me interrupt. Aunt Emily, the food here is really very good ...'

'Oh, Cedric, food, yes, I know. And some of the people I saw in the East End hadn't had a square meal for months.'

A waiter came from the street entrance, bent to speak to a diner near the door and, with a triumphant glance around this enemy place, went out. The man whom the waiter had spoken to held up his hand. 'We came from next door. From the Last Word. He says there is news that the battle at Kosovo ended last night. It's a big victory for the Serbs.'

'Surely,' said Cedric, addressing everyone, 'it ought to be called a draw because battles at Kosovo will certainly break out again.'

At this some people shouted at him. There wasn't a note of mockery in it, as there had been on the pavement.

A group of young men got up from the back of the restaurant and advanced on Cedric.

'Good Lord,' said Cedric. 'A lynch mob.'

The proprietor came running forward, waved back the threatening young men and said to Cedric, 'Sir, in your own interests, do please leave,' and he indicated Fiona's flagrant cheeks under the Serbian locks.

Cedric got up, pulled up Fiona, and Emily got up too.

'Never mind,' said Cedric. 'I know a good place just near here.' And with one arm around Emily, the other around Fiona, he steered them out of Turkish Delights.

On the pavement the Serbian supporters were whooping and dancing.

'No, Fiona,' said Cedric, 'come away. Everyone knows you are a Serbie.' And he took them down the street to a restaurant where he was known.

'Aunt Emily,' said Fiona, 'I am a serious person. Please believe me.'

Next day at Emily's hotel, Cedric said that Fiona was mortified and desolate, he hoped Emily could see – and he was here to assure her that Fiona was as sensible a girl as anyone could wish.

'Cedric,' said Emily, 'don't you understand? I have been making plans thinking of me, and of my old friend Daisy, and perhaps one or two others, but here I am with you – and we have only recently got to know each other, and now there's Fiona and —'

'But, Aunt Emily, you can't possibly imagine you can do all

you plan with just you and one or two others. For one thing, you'll need a secretary.'

'I'll think about it all,' said Emily.

'But not for too long,' said Cedric.

At once a letter arrived from Daisy, saying that two houses were going for a song not far from the one she and Emily had shared: Rupert had bought them for this new venture. At once Cedric arrived, and again, Emily having opened her house, the two sat at the great table in the dining-room.

'And now, Aunt Emily!'

'Daisy doesn't want to be bothered with business things: she's getting married. You must make the people involved, Daisy, her Rupert, me, you ...'

'And Fiona, I hope?'

'Very well.'

'You won't be sorry. She's such a good girl. I simply cannot believe my luck, getting her.'

And so it was, and Emily found herself very busy.

And very alone. Daisy was in the throes of 'flowers and fuss'. So was Fiona.

Emily, alone in her big house, stared hard into her mirror and told herself that she was sad not because she wasn't getting married but because she believed she had never been married, not really. She compared herself and William with Daisy and Rupert – 'But they are really fond of each other,' whispered Emily, thinking that this was a stern face looking back at her. She contrasted it with Daisy's, all smiles these days, and when she thought of the young couple, Cedric and

Fiona, tears definitely threatened. Just imagine her William joking and teasing, like Cedric – not to be thought of! Those two couples, one middle-aged, one so young, were both inside a kind of happiness Emily had never known. And so, Emily admonished her face, bleak enough, in the reflected light from the glass, there was something wrong with her. There must be. Cedric said that Fiona was 'such fun'. Daisy wrote that 'I am so happy, Emily, and never expected to be.'

But luckily there was plenty of work to do.

Cedric dropped in with documents, plans, ideas. 'It's lucky, Aunt Emily, that nothing much is expected of a bridegroom. Poor Fiona.'

'Cedric, I am getting letters by every post. Do we really want to staff our schools with society girls?'

'I hope you are not calling Fiona a society girl, Aunt Emily.'

'Look, Cedric.' She pushed towards him a heap of the letters.

'I'll take these. I'm bound to know most of them. I'll make sure you choose right.'

And, again, 'Cedric, surely we don't need so many bishops.'

'You can never have too many bishops. We'll just choose the fanciest for our letterhead.'

He asked her to write down, in a paragraph, how she visualized their project in five years' time – and ten years' time. He said, 'William left you a tidy sum, Aunt Emily, but not enough to pay for all you are planning. No, I'll draft you a nice little charity. We must have bishops for that. Archbishops would be better. And perhaps a royal or two. I tell you who we must have to run all that. Fiona's cousin, Madge. She's really a whiz at all things charitable.'

How very odd, Emily thought. It's a question of schools and books for the poor, and suddenly I spend all my time with Lady this and the Honourable that, not to mention tea with bishops.

Daisy got herself wed, Fiona did too, and in no time the girl was Emily's right hand, always there, responsible, clever, everything Emily could have wished.

Then, the young couple's new house having fallen through, Emily let Cedric and Fiona her house, keeping a room for herself. But she liked better her flat in the house in Beak Street.

Within six months, the first William Martin-White school was open, and already a great success.

After the first school was opened, Mary Lane often came to London, though at first she was shocked by what she saw, the unhealthy little children of the East End: 'We do have poverty in the country, yes,' she said, 'but I've never seen anything as bad as this.' She stayed with Emily, when she was there, but there was a good bit of travelling to be done: requests for information about these Martin-White schools came from other cities. And soon there was a bonus, because Daisy, now the fuss and flowers were over, came often to observe and to help when she could. She planned to retire soon, so intriguing did she find the schools. Then Harold retired, and he too visited London, though never without saying how shocking he found it, a feverish, hysterical place. He had a 'lair' in

Rupert and Daisy's house and there he and Rupert might sit to discuss the world and its affairs. Though not often, for Rupert was so busy.

Mary Lane told Emily that 'the two wives', which was how she described Betsy and Phyllis, had set up a school, and it was doing well, using all kinds of tips from the Martin-White schools – there were soon three in London alone.

Why did not the Longerfield school ask to be a Martin-White school? They did, and were refused: a stipulation was that there must be a Montessori teacher in every accredited school.

'Well, never mind,' said Mary. 'It's a good little school and I am sure you would think so. So, come down and see it.'

She did not press, and Emily might have wondered why. Something had happened that involved her, and perhaps it would be better, people decided, if she did not know about it. And she never did know: this was a credit to everyone's discretion.

Bert, who really couldn't stand Emily, though he wouldn't have been able to say why, had taken to mocking her storytelling – the mice and the cat and the birds, and so on. He mimicked her well, and people laughed at his 'And then the dear little rats ate up all the cats and soon the mice …' and so on. The venom of his dislike for Emily made his mockery upsetting to her friends, and he was asked to desist, but he did not. And then the surprising thing happened. Some small children, hearing Bert's rather nasty mimicry, did not 'take in' that this was criticism of their dear aunt Emily, and cried out,

'Uncle Bert is telling stories, he is telling stories. Tell us a story, Uncle Bert ...'

Bert was quite affronted, then shooed them away and even physically went away himself, to the end of the farm, but as soon as he reappeared, it began, 'Here's Uncle Bert, tell us a story ...'

'And now,' said his wife, Phyllis, 'you aren't going to be able to get out of this one, are you, Bert?'

Alfred, at first, laughed, for it was funny, this clumsy, shambling man, who had always seemed to be in the act of turning away from whomever he spoke to, or from a situation. How could he turn away from these children – two of them his own, all of whom he had known since they were born?

'Well,' said Alfred to Bert, 'why don't you have a shot at it, then? They aren't a critical audience.'

Bert could not bring himself to descend to mice and cats but there were horses now on the farm, and he tried to make up tales about them. But he really didn't have the knack. The children were indulgent: they sat around him, mouths open, eyes expectant always for the magic of Aunt Emily. And Bert could not do it. He simply could not.

He would say, 'You know that new horse, Grey Boy? Well, we bought him at Doncaster for fifty pounds but he isn't worth that. He can't keep his pace.'

'A story,' shouted the children. 'A story, Uncle Bert.'

Mary Lane rescued Bert with gifts of children's books she brought from London. Bert would arrive at the school after the children's lunch and their nap, and read to them. At first he could not prevent his voice deriding the simple tales, but the children knew he was doing this and said, 'Not like that. Read it properly.'

This went on quite well, and Bert was kept at it by his wife and by Alfred and Betsy.

And then, as had happened before, he had 'a bit of a relapse' – as Mary told Emily.

'Yes, we did keep it up very well, but something got to him – we don't know what – and he was off, and Betsy took him in hand again, but this time it's Alfred too. Alfred and Bert are such friends, they could be brothers, and Alfred nearly went berserk when he found Bert drunk in a ditch outside the pub. Betsy told Bert he had to go back to reading to the children – though some of us are wondering if all those children pestering him didn't set him off. So he and Alfred are in our school every afternoon, reading to the children.'

'Alfred is?' Emily couldn't grasp this at all.

'It is a question of keeping Bert at it, do you see? Alfred finds him, wherever he is on the farm, and takes him to the school, and chooses what stories, and he reads, turn by turn with Bert, to the children. And Betsy drops in, too, and sometimes she reads. And so we do need a lot of books. I'd like it if you could donate some, the same as you have for the schools.'

Emily went to her chief suppliers, ordered them to send a good selection of children's books to Longerfield, and went down herself. She stayed with Mary, as usual, and slept in the room where she had slept so often, with Daisy in the other bed. The little blue enamel candlestick was there, in its proper place, and she lit it to watch the shadows move on the low ceiling where a knot-hole in a beam, or a spider's web, could set off ideas and – when she needed them – stories for the children. Was it the same spider up there, a tiny blotch on the edge of its web? She liked to think so. She liked to think of this room as her real bedroom, this bed her own. These days she was so often in a new room, yet another bed, in towns she did not know, that a little spider's web, spread in the corner, seemed like an assurance that she, too, Emily McVeagh, had something steady and reliable in her. Her life seemed to have been a series of adjustments to arbitrary pressures.

She was in the Redways' big sitting-room, where she had been before to assess the musical capacities of Michael and Tom, but they were not there today; there were no children present. Present, quite forcefully, was Mr Redway: Mary referred to him these days as 'old Mr Redway'. Did that mean Bert was young Mr Redway? Mrs Redway, about the time of Bert's last relapse, had decided one morning that there was no point in getting up and had been in bed ever since. On the whole people were relieved, but there was a lot of work for Bert's wife, who was a handsome dark woman with a high colour and a sharp, enquiring look. Betsy sat near her, a large, pretty, fair woman, who sighed as she sat and fanned herself: it was a warm July afternoon. Mary, invited, said she could not come because Bert was convinced she 'had it in for him'. She knew the atmosphere would be fraught and did not want to make it worse.

A tea tray stood ready but Emily noted it was not until Mr

Redway nodded at Phyllis that she began to pour.

Bert seemed annoyed at the business of teacups and kept saying impatiently, 'Well, let's get down to it.'

Emily had a fair idea what 'it' would be, but she was discommoded by Bert's hostility to her. And yet he did not seem a belligerent person. He wore a loose dark shirt, popular because it was 'army surplus' from Vienna. But he looked like an old dog, who was in the habit of growling at everyone. She had no idea how much he disliked her.

Alfred was still a tall, well-made man, holding himself straight, and he was wearing a jacket chosen by his wife because she said the material was like a thrush's feathers, dark brown with lightish touches.

Both men wore the army boots that could be purchased anywhere these days for a few pounds.

'I want to pick a bone with you,' said Bert, direct to Emily, waving away a teacup, sugar and milk.

Now, Emily was prepared for this because Mary had told her to be. 'Well, then,' said she, agreeably. 'Let's have it.'

'I want an explanation – I mean, we want an explanation …' Here he hastily indicated his wife and Betsy. 'We want to know why you won't let the Longerfield school be one of your outfits?'

'You see,' began Emily, holding her own – just – against the force of his hostility, 'didn't they tell you when you applied? There has to be a Montessori teacher for it to be a Martin-White school.'

'Don't you have the say about what happens? Isn't it your money, then?' demanded Bert, leaning towards her, his fists clenched tight.

'You see,' said Emily, 'if we were using only my money, then we would have enough for, let's say, four or five schools. It's not just a question of setting them up; we have to maintain them, pay salaries, all that kind of thing.'

'Well, then? Well, then?' urged Bert, dismissing what she had already said.

'But to do what we are doing now – and we have fifteen schools, with more on the way – it couldn't be my money. It has to be a charity. And then you have dos and don'ts ...' and Emily could not prevent her impatience at these restrictions showing. 'If you didn't have some sort of rules, then just anybody could decide to call themselves a Martin-White school.'

'Just anybody!' said Phyllis, angry.

'Well, we're glad to know at last what we are,' said Betsy.

Bert was grinning with the triumph of the moment. Emily was sitting there, limp, hurt, and as much by the sudden antagonism as by what they had said.

'Whoa,' said Alfred, 'wait a minute. You've brought a whole lot of books for us – Emily,' he said. After all, they had known each other for a quarter of a century.

'Yes, but I paid for them myself,' said Emily, addressing him direct, ignoring the others, whom she felt as enemies just then.

'You mean,' said Bert, 'that your precious foundation,

or whatever you call it, couldn't even fork out for a few books?'

'No,' said Emily. 'But I have. And I have arranged for the bookshop to send you more.'

'Well, then, Emily,' said Alfred – and she could see that he was deliberately rescuing her from Bert's real rage, 'I'm going to put in a private request. My boys – do you remember them, perhaps? – they like to read, but how about some Bulldog Drummond or Henty, or Edgar Wallace? They are well beyond fairies and little animals. And I like that kind of reading too. Or Tarzan, perhaps. And I always did fancy Zane Grey.'

'I'll see to it,' said Emily, smiling gratefully, and looking straight at him. 'Of course. And we were thinking of expanding a bit anyway – adult books as well. Because when we set up our little libraries, the adults always ask, What about us, then?'

'There you are,' said Alfred. 'So, I am not alone. Our boys will be really pleased, won't they, Betsy?'

'Yes,' said Betsy, knowing she was part of a rescue of Bert – something that had so often to be done.

'And now,' said Alfred, 'it's time for us to be looking at the horses, isn't it, Bert?' And he pulled Bert up by the arm.

'If you say so,' said Bert, deflated, apparently defeated, his anger gone.

As he and Alfred went out, Bert said, over his shoulder, 'And thanks for the books you brought. Thanks a lot.' Alfred had nudged him.

The two men went off to the stables.

The two wives said, quite nicely now that Bert had taken himself off, 'We'll show you our school, anyway.'

'We're proud of it.'

An empty labourer's cottage made the schoolhouse, and this afternoon it was being well patronized, as Emily and Mary could see, walking along dusty lanes towards it. A great ash shaded it, and children of all ages were playing in the cool, and the two women stopped talking because of their babble. Then, some of the older ones recognized Emily and called out, 'Are you coming to tell us stories? Are you?' And they entered the building in a crowd of children.

Betsy and Phyllis were with about thirty, pouring out lemonade from great china jugs. Every kind of glass, tumbler and cup was being used, and Emily thought that there was always a battle in her schools because 'they', the trustees, whom she thought of collectively as 'the debs', were always wanting to buy the most expensive cups and glasses to be had while Emily and Fiona tried to keep costs down.

Emily and Mary were given cups of lemonade and sat on a windowsill to observe. These children were really young, some babies with their mothers in tow. Older children, girls and boys, were in an adjoining room. They were reading stories to their age group. The small children had Phyllis and Betsy reading to them. Those who had recognized Emily pressed around her, but Emily was a long way, these days, from mice in pantries and the adventures of blackbirds. She found a book from the piles she had brought, and read to them about the feats of a kitten called Thomas Widgeon.

'More! More! More!' and she went on, while half listening to the bigger children's voices next door, reading *The Jungle Book.*

Some of the very smallest fell asleep. It was hot. This pleasantest of afternoons went smoothly along, interrupted when a girl brought cakes, biscuits and milk on trays from the big house. Mr Redway dropped in to sit with Emily and Mary and watch.

Emily felt that this school, the friendliness and ease of it, was what her schools were missing. In an interval of reading she said sorrowfully, 'Plans don't always turn out the way we think they will.'

'What do you mean?' said Mary.

'This, here, is better than any of the schools I've done.'

'But, Emily, how can you compare them? Don't you see? Everyone here, we all know each other.'

'Is that what it is? I wonder. And there isn't a qualified teacher, but it seems to me Phyllis and Betsy do well enough.'

'And I come sometimes,' said Mr Redway. 'And don't forget Bert and Alfred.'

'I feel that I've missed something; something's lacking with us.'

Mary, who had seen all the schools, except a couple of the newest in the Midlands, said, 'Emily, that's absurd. The Martin-White schools are what everyone wants to emulate. You must know that.'

Emily was silent, because she did not know how to express what she felt, which was – perhaps? – this was a sort of family, everybody seemed to belong together, there was a kindliness – was that it? And it was what she had always missed in every place but Longerfield.

Emily saw Bert and Alfred walking through the children near the tree, but then Bert, seeing her, swerved off and Alfred went with him.

Emily could not miss it: Bert did not want to meet her.

'Bert is very odd, isn't he?' she said, thoroughly uncomfortable, to Mary.

'Very strange indeed,' instantly agreed Mary. 'And I am sure that we all of us do wonder what would have happened if Alfred and Betsy – and Phyllis, of course – weren't so wonderful with him.'

Then it was getting late, and the smaller children went off with the bigger ones, and soon Phyllis and Betsy, and a couple of girls from the big house, were clearing away the lemonade and the milk, and Emily and Mary tried to help.

'No, you run along,' said 'the wives'. 'But we hope you weren't too shocked by our country ways.'

Emily, of course, denied she felt any such thing, but could not say what she did feel.

They left the schoolhouse, went through the deep shade of the ash, where some older children still played, and were in the yellow glare of a lowering sun.

'There seem to be quite a few empty cottages,' remarked Emily, and heard that 'With this new machinery, many fewer workers are needed on the farms.' And there they were, the machines, standing together in a big field, making sharp black shadows.

Beyond the field of machines there was a large pond where stood a dozen horses with the water lapping about their legs and, in one or two cases, their sides.

'There are half as many people on the Redway farm,' said Mary, 'and it is true of all the farms round about.'

They stopped to watch the horses, and their enjoyment of the cool water, and went on through fields that were red with dust.

'We joke that there is more of Longerfield in the air above us than there is on the ground.'

'Doesn't that matter?'

'There's nothing it seems we can do, anyway,' said Mary. 'All of us older ones care but the young ones don't seem able to see what is happening.'

They passed some young men, all with Surplus badges on their chests.

At supper they discussed how the young men were going off to London and signing up with recruiters for service in the wars that were going on, in South America, Africa and parts of Asia.

'At least not here,' said Mary.

The parents of Longerfield were afraid because of their sons wanting to be soldiers, and Emily asked about Alfred and Betsy's boys.

'They are a bit too young yet – but not for long.'

And next morning Mary called Emily to see, through a window, two people in the lane. Two tall, broad boys took up all the space beneath the trees. They were throwing a cricket ball back and forth to each other, as they strode along.

'If you were a recruiter and those two came and said they were eighteen, would you believe them?'

'If I wanted to,' said Emily.

'But they are not quite sixteen. The work they do with the horses puts on years and muscle. There's nothing the parents can do. Of course, they love the horses.'

What happened was this: Bert had for years asked his father to breed horses, which were his passion. Mr Redway said he didn't want all the bother, when farming was getting difficult anyway. Alfred told Mr Redway that it would be good for Bert to have his horses. 'You see, it'd be something of his own, some-thing he does.' He didn't have to say that Bert did not have a special role on the farm. Bert joked that he was the children's father, so 'I'm good for something, then.'

Disused stables were brought back into use, and a race-course made. And from that moment none of the boys could be kept away from the horses and their needs. Some of the girls were as attracted.

But Alfred had been heard to say that giving Bert his heart's desire had given him bad nights: all the boys on the farm grew heavier, larger, stronger, with all their work for the horses, feeding them, exercising them – stable lads in all but name.

'Poor Alfred, poor Betsy,' said Mary. 'Everybody feels for

them. A lot of our lads have already gone off to the wars, a couple of the girls, too – as nurses.'

That evening, as the sun grew large and red in its veil of dust, Mary handed Emily a hat and the two went up to the horses. It seemed everyone Emily had ever seen in Longerfield was there, crowding the rails, or taking horses to the big pond.

Alfred was watching where the horses came in after a gallop. A big man. No lightweight. He had been riding a tall bulky black horse, which stood near him while he fondled its neck and ears. He was looking down the track to where a man on a horse came fast towards them in a cloud of dust. It was Bert. Never had Emily seen or heard of Bert without there being an edge of disapprobation on faces, in voices. She had never seen or imagined this Bert. He was smiling, at ease, confident, and as he came near Alfred, he wheeled, jumped off the horse, and vaulted the rail to stand near him.

'The fastest yet,' said Alfred. 'Well done! So, you'll go to Doncaster next weekend, then?'

'I might as well,' said Bert, bowing slightly, a sardonic little acknowledgement of the applause from stable boys, the watching children and some parents.

So, that was Bert, thought Emily. Would she have ever imagined he could be this hero, basking in applause, in approval?

And, she thought, that is what happened to me. Suddenly I found I could tell tales and the children were after me, 'More, Aunt Emily. Tell us more.'

She looked towards Bert, smiling, feeling the warmth of her approval for him – for herself – and he saw her, and extended his little bow to include her.

Then, he looked at her, and his grin was openly satirical. It was what she wore: she was catching the evening train to London in an hour, and she was dressed for London, not Longerfield. She had on a dark-blue linen coat and skirt, and the white collar and belt were reddened with dust. She tried to brush it off, making things worse.

Ignoring Bert, though she did look embarrassed, she said to Alfred, 'I won't forget what you said. I'll get the books sent directly to you.'

'Then thanks,' he said, smiling straight at her, in a way he had – direct, personal, really seeing her.

Here was the kindliness that she felt she was missing every-where but in this place, had always missed – had not known that she missed.

He was a kind man, yes, someone to be trusted. His face clouded, his eyes were troubled: he was now looking at his two lads, big lads, who seemed so very much older than their years. Both held a horse by its bridle and both leaped up and rode off, no saddle, just the reins to hold on to.

And now his eyes were full of tears.

'Well,' he said to her, steadying his voice, 'I expect Mary has told you of our worry. It's not much comfort to know that most of the parents around here share it.'

And he went in through a little gate and swung himself up on to the great horse.

'See you again, I expect,' he said to Emily, riding off, while Bert rode beside him.

Emily left Longerfield, as always, sadly, and found herself thinking she could retire there, buy a little house near Mary, never have to leave Longerfield again. And she was amazed at herself: retire! And it was such a success, people applying in droves to work with them, people giving them money – and that was the point. It had needed Emily McVeagh to start the thing, but it could go on nicely without her. Fiona would be just as efficient … She was going to see Fiona now. She believed that Fiona was the luckiest thing that could have happened. Emily had her flat in Beak Street, could always stay with Daisy, but she had lost her room in her own house: Fiona had not asked her, but it was evident the room was needed for a nanny, who was starting today. Fiona had accomplished two children, apparently without effort, and this had not stopped her working with Emily. But a nanny had become essential. Emily wanted to see how it was working. And she loved being there at the children's bedtime.

She went straight to the nursery, which had once been hers and William's bedroom, and found Fiona sitting by a lively fire, her first little girl standing clinging to the bars of a cot and watching her mother feed the new baby.

Emily wanted to hear what Fiona would say about events in Longerfield: she relied on her for a kind of clarity, so she told herself. Really, Fiona agreed so well with Emily about everything, it was not till Emily had been confirmed, as it were, by Fiona, that she felt she could face her critics, 'the debs and the bishops' – most of whom seemed to be Fiona's cousins or some other kind of relative.

She watched Fiona's confident clasp of her babe, saw the round full white breast, which seemed to be like a different aspect of Fiona, not known to her: she knew well a quick, clever, ambitious girl, impatient of checks and obstacles; the soft round breast spoke of other capacities. Emily told Fiona of her visit to Longerfield, taking her time, watching Fiona's face, which showed she had grasped at once everything Emily had said. In just one part of the narrative Emily was not sure of conveying what she felt: sitting in the schoolhouse with all those children, and feeling a rightness there, which she would have liked Fiona to share.

Fiona's eyes were on Emily's face as she talked and then, as the visit to the schoolhouse was about to end, she said, showing she had caught what Emily had not said, or felt that there was more Emily would like to say, 'Some day I must come with you to Longerfield because you come back from it so – contented.'

'Contented?'

'Yes. But there's one thing that stands out. Whenever we set up a library for a school, we are always asked about books for adults.' Now Emily listed the novels Alfred had requested, and added more she had thought of since.

'Yes,' said Fiona. 'It seems to me we might have a separate fund for the grown-up books.'

'There are libraries,' said Emily, 'but if we have little

libraries of our own, or even lists we could put up, I feel they would know what to ask for in the public libraries. They don't know what there is, you see, what's available.'

'I know just the person for that,' said Fiona. 'She's longing to work with us. Her name is Jessie and I'll speak to her. No, she won't want to be paid.'

'That's one advantage of the debs,' said Emily.

'To have some work … the poor things,' said Fiona. 'Everywhere women going mad, wanting to work.'

The babe at her breast seemed to fall off it, as if his mouth had been the grasp of a limpet. He lay, hands curled, eyes shut, on Fiona's lap. Fiona looked down over the swollen breast at this replete infant. Her breast budded drops of milk. A black and white cat beside the fire miaowed. Fiona deftly picked up a saucer near it, allowed some milk to fall into it and put it down by the cat, which, like the baby, seemed pleased. The infant in her cot was sinking back and down, and was lying, blinking sleepily, silent.

'All fed,' said Fiona. 'The cat was here long before Rosie. It was jealous and I was afraid it might harm Rosie. One day when I finished feeding, the cat jumped on my lap and licked my breast so I put down a saucer of milk and the cat stopped being jealous.'

'I wonder if the cat thinks it's a baby or a kitten?' said Emily.

'I mustn't let Miss Burton see me give my milk to the cat,' said Fiona. Mimicking a hoity-toity voice, she said, "'The cat'll get ideas above its station. You don't want that." She's already told the cook I'm a real Bohemian, but she thinks she can get me back in line.'

'I wish you were coming with me to Scotland,' said Emily.

'So do I. Well, nursery days won't be for ever.'

A knock, and a large, matronly woman appeared, who said to Fiona, 'Give me the baby. I'll take him for tonight. I'll give him a bottle if he wakes. And now you must get to bed early, you really can't go on without some sleep.'

In this way Emily learned of the hardships of nursery days. The nanny lifted the sleeping baby, pulled a little blanket over the older infant, and left, while Fiona sat yawning in the firelight.

Another knock. The cook appeared. 'Dinner is served,' she said, and to Emily, whom she knew, 'I've laid a place for you, madam.'

The two women descended the stairs.

In the dining-room, where there was now a smaller round table supplementing the vast one of Emily's reign, Cedric sat yawning.

'We are ordered to go to bed, Cedric,' said Fiona, and he said, 'Aunt Emily, thank you for letting us have your room. If Fiona and I hadn't Miss Burton to keep us in order I don't think we would survive.'

He sat at the table, Fiona near him. Food arrived, and was not much eaten.

'I don't have to eat,' said Cedric, 'but poor Fiona does.'

'Yes, you do,' said Fiona. 'I am sure Miss Burton would not hear of your not eating.'

He accomplished a few mouthfuls and retired to a little green sofa that Emily had once been fond of. He sat and yawned. Fiona, eating as if Miss Burton stood over her, took in sole as if it were medicine and went to sit by Cedric who put his arms around her.

'I am sure you have already worked it out, Aunt Emily,' said Cedric, 'but if we are going to have a third child then Miss Burton is absolutely essential.'

'Well, are you?'

'We haven't decided,' said Cedric, kissing Fiona. Emily felt that Miss Burton probably would not have approved this kiss and the others that followed.

Not too tired to flirt, thought Emily, musing, If married couples do flirt – well, I and William certainly didn't.

'But if we haven't got the energy simply to go upstairs to bed,' said Cedric, 'then is it likely we have enough energy for a third child?'

Fiona murmured: a joke, Emily thought. Cedric laughed out loud, and said something that Emily knew was pretty sexual, but she did not know what he was really saying.

The two, Cedric and Fiona, seemed to drowse in each other's arms, kissing a little, then some more – and in came Miss Burton, surveying them with severity.

'You two must really go and get some sleep,' said Miss Burton. 'You'll lose your milk,' she warned Fiona.

'And what will I lose?' enquired Cedric, seriously. 'Very well, Fiona, up you get.'

He pulled her up, and she stood resting against him, already half asleep.

'That's right,' said Miss Burton. She nodded at Emily, and went out.

'Good night, then, Emily,' murmured Fiona.

'Good night, dear Aunt Emily,' said Cedric, and the two left the scene.

Emily did not believe that sleep was on their immediate agenda.

Emily found a cab, got to Beak Street, and lay awake thinking of how she would get the books Alfred wanted to him quickly.

When Emily heard of a storyteller somewhere, she went to see him or her at once, and she was going to see a certain Alistair McTaggart, who lived in a village near Stirling. It was quite a journey, and she did a good deal of work on the train. She did not know what she would find. Some of the old storytellers behaved as if they were guardians of a store of gold, quickly diminished if used recklessly; others responded to invitations to visit schools and tell stories to small children. This Alistair was a tall, craggy, whiskery man who at once said that to introduce children to the great tradition was more important than anything. He was famous locally, in many pubs, was invited to ceilidhs and gatherings, and invited Emily to go with him that very night to a nearby pub where he was expected.

This meant she would have to stay the night in Stirling, though he offered her a bed in what he called a spare room, which was a tiny space, not more than a large cupboard, off his main room. She did not at all mind the meagreness of the space, but thought that it would be late after the pub, perhaps he – or she – might be tight, and surely … But in the event the taxi to take her to Stirling was cancelled, because it was indeed late, both were pretty tight – they had sung and told stories till nearly morning.

Emily, pressured by Alistair, had told a story inspired by Fiona's cat, though the milk that staved off jealousy was cow's milk. She was happy to fall into bed in her cubbyhole of a room and to enjoy a vast Scottish breakfast with Alistair. She could have stayed another day or two – she was invited – but had to return to London. *Had* to? Why?

She told Fiona about this wonder of a storyteller, who kept a crowded pub silent for hours with his repertoire of traditional tales, and Fiona made an excuse to go up and hear Alistair McTaggart at work in the Martin-White school in Edinburgh. It was not easy for her to stay a night, or many, as invited, because of her infants, so she returned reluctantly to London and her duties.

A conversation took place between her and Emily, soon after.

Having said how much she had enjoyed Alistair McTaggart, and her experience watching him, listening to him, with the children, she remarked, casually though, that she thought Alistair was intrigued by Emily. That was how she put it. Did

Emily seem conscious that more was meant? She did seem on her guard, and did not look at Fiona, who then spoke very low, so that Emily could pretend she had not heard. 'He really likes you, Emily, but really.'

Emily had heard, but was silent, her eyes down – was she blushing? – and then she said, laughing, 'Well, I like him too.'

Fiona, encouraged, asked, 'Have you thought of marrying again, Emily?'

Emily said, 'You know, Fiona, not every marriage is like yours and Cedric's.'

At once Fiona said, 'Oh, I do know, believe me. I know how lucky I am.'

'And isn't Cedric lucky too?'

'Not as much.'

Emily showed that she needed to hear more, and obliging Fiona gave her what she craved with 'A good man is hard to find.'

And hadn't Emily herself proved the rightness of this pronouncement?

'When I check with my friends, Aunt Emily, believe me, I do know my luck.'

Fiona was still looking enquiringly at Emily. She seemed now rather like an earnest little girl, even more so because she was wearing her hair in two fair plaits. She only wore these indoors. Soon after the first baby was born she was out and about with her hair plaited and even with little baby bows. This was for convenience: she did not go in for 'Serb' or 'Turk' hairdos. Friends, seeing her, instantly announced a new trend: 'Pigtails for Peace' was the craze, but Fiona scorned to approve it.

'You know, Aunt Emily, we – that is, Cedric and I – think it is too soon for you to decide on being an old maid.'

Emily had to laugh at this but there was no doubt she was troubled; no laughing matter, her face said, and then she asked, 'But shouldn't one be young to think of getting married?'

Fiona clearly did not know what to say, but she was thinking: Aunt Emily wasn't exactly old when she married Uncle William. And Emily was thinking: I wouldn't marry William now, whatever age I was. She simply could not discuss with Fiona just how much of a disappointment William had been. She had never told anybody. Fiona discussed her marriage with her friends, did she? Emily could not imagine doing that.

'You haven't thought it out, Fiona. Am I going to live in a little village in Scotland, just like that, and give up my work?'

Now Fiona was silent, partly because she realized just how very much she would miss Emily.

Soon she remarked that there would be trouble again with the debs. The two, Emily and Fiona, enjoyed their ongoing battles with the debs, which had become partly invented too. This time it was that the debs would say there was no need to spend so much on Alistair McTaggart's engagement to 'tell fairytales', as they put it, in Edinburgh, Glasgow and Stirling. The debs always contested any money spent on the story-tellers: it was amazing how this was always being crowded out of any curriculum. Fiona and Emily fought their good fight, Emily remembering that this was where the whole great airy structure of schools and boards and trusts had begun: she had told funny little tales to some children in Longerfield and had been followed by crowds of them: 'Tell us a story.'

And so the subject of Alistair McTaggart was dropped, but messages came from him, saying how much he looked forward to Mistress McVeagh's next visit; she had told him that her maiden name surely must mean she had a Scottish claim somewhere and he called her Mistress McVeagh. Between Fiona and Emily it was understood, without anything being said, that if Emily wasn't so very busy she would certainly spend more time up there with Alistair McTaggart, for, as Fiona reminded her, with a smile, 'He loves you, Emily; he does, you know.'

Then he would telephone Fiona to say he was expecting Mistress McVeagh for the ceilidh next week. 'I am counting on you, Fiona.' And, more often than not, Emily did go. She became known as Alistair McTaggart's friend from London, who was a storyteller in her own right. And all this went on, pleasantly enough, for a year, two, three – until one day Alistair rang Fiona to say he was not himself, he was poorly, would Mistress McVeagh perhaps come and see to him?

Up went Emily to find him in bed, fevered, but with heavy sweats, coughing, and very much not himself. She telephoned Fiona to say she must stay and watch over Alistair, to whom she had already called the doctor, who agreed with her that Mr McTaggart was not at all well. And then, one night, Emily found him dying: it was his heart that was doing him in. He died, and Emily, having alerted his daughter to attend to the arrangements, went weeping to London. But she had to go back to Scotland for the funeral.

She learned from the people there that she would always be welcome if she returned for visits; and Emily wept again. She said to Fiona that she seemed to do little else. 'And I'm *not* a weeper,' she protested.

As soon as Alistair McTaggart was buried Daisy rang to say her father had died. The funeral was next week.

'It never rains but it pours,' said Emily; and the two deaths were only part of it.

On the whole, the Martin-White schools had gone along without much difficulty. Nothing very bad had happened, except for a fire, which burned nobody; the insurance, instructed by Cedric, paid up. And there had been a bit of trouble with tramps using a school in Cornwall as shelter.

But now it seemed as if a quarter of a century's accumulated bile was exploding over the name, the reputation, the very aims of the Martin-White schools. A teacher became pregnant, and before she could be unobtrusively got rid of, the press heard of it and there were headlines along the lines of 'A Wolf in Sheep's Clothing'; 'Martin-White Schools Shelter Immorality'; 'Free Love Flourishes in the Martin-White Foundation'.

For some reason the fierce moralities of the time had been touched off by this case, of a pretty girl called Ivy Smith who, like thousands of girls before her – fair-minded people were pointing out – found themselves in the family way before they'd got a ring on their finger. There was no chance of Ivy getting a ring – her so-called fiancé had disappeared. Emily was, as it happened, visiting Scotland, and Fiona was on holiday with her children in the country. Daisy simply sacked the girl, and advised her to apply to such and such a convent. Emily and Fiona, hearing of this, told Daisy she was harsh; Fiona even used the word 'hypocritical'. 'We can't have illegitimate babies in our schools,' said Daisy. 'Didn't you see what the papers said?'

The trustees (the debs and the bishops), as Fiona said, put their collective feet down and threatened resignations, public scandals, letters to *The Times*.

'We can't have it,' insisted Daisy, who was suspected by Emily of taking too much personal relish in this. People were remembering that Daisy Lane had spent years of her life examining girls not only for skills in nursing but for behaviour, reputation, conduct, morals.

'There is nothing we can do,' said Cedric, who thoroughly disapproved of how Ivy had been treated. 'It will blow over. We can be sure of that.'

Next thing, there was an article in one of the more sensational newspapers about how girls looked after by the nuns of that convent were treated. 'Nothing like it has been heard of since Dickens'; 'Conditions that would have been condemned in a Victorian workhouse'. And so on.

Ivy, who had visited Longerfield and had become friends with the Redway women, was rescued from the convent, and invited to teach at the Longerfield school.

'Well,' said Emily to Fiona, and with the kind of grim humour not everyone appreciated, 'the Longerfield school has its Montessori-trained teacher at last.'

No sooner had Emily returned to London from the funeral of Harold than there came a letter signed by Betsy Tayler, Phyllis Redway, and a separate letter from Mary Lane:

Emily, I don't think you realize how much resentment – I think I may say, real anger – was caused by your dismissal of Ivy, and sending her off to that really dreadful place. I went to see the conditions there. I have myself written a letter to *The Times* about it. It is a disgrace that such a place should exist and – I presume – get public money. I believe the convent is a charity. I do think it would be a help if you could come down and explain. I simply do not believe that you would be so heartless as to condemn a girl to such a shocking place.

Emily wrote to Mary to say that she had had nothing to do with the treatment of Ivy; and knew that Mary would see that this message was transmitted to the others. All the same, she might not be personally responsible, but responsibility she did have – some. And there was another thought niggling away. When she had heard first that this girl had got pregnant and there was no chance of a wedding, she had found herself thinking, What a nuisance. How very badly timed. And, Imagine that a baby could dislodge all our arrangements ...

They were negotiating a deal that would spread the foundation's work into Wales and into Scotland. A scandal would easily put an end to that. Suddenly there were complications and difficulties where before there had been none. A baby. Just one baby. A 'love-child', they called it ... So Emily had fulminated, admittedly, only to herself, her ill-temper kept private and not admitted even to Fiona. And now she was ashamed of herself. She, who had 'swooned and mooned' – as she put it – over Fiona's infants, being so censorious over an illegitimate child.

The train from London must be late: people waiting for Emily were on their second and third cups of tea.

Who was waiting? Not Mr Redway, who had said he was too old to get excited because some silly girl had a bun in the oven. He sat outside the long windows, in a chair, bundled up: there was a sharp little wind. Ivy was very much there, centre stage, the baby in a basket beside her. Mrs Redway was dead, having gone presumably to her Maker, where she had told everyone for years she was heading. Alfred, who had not much changed, was there, with Bert beside him, who had got fat and blowsy: his hand shook as he lifted a teacup. Betsy, the fair-sized matron, sat with Phyllis, a sharp-nosed, dark woman. If this gathering had been only a week ago, the self-congratulatory complacency of the two wives would have been quite intolerable – but events were moving fast.

What had not changed was Ivy's readiness to tell her tale, again and ... 'Oh, not again,' Bert had complained.

She had indeed just gone through the recital, but concluded with 'Yes, I know that Mrs Martin-White had nothing to do with it – but she was off with her fancy man in Scotland.'

At this Alfred, suddenly angry, said to her, and it sounded like an explosion of emotion, 'Not well said, from a girl whose fancy man wasn't up to much.'

'But well named,' said Ivy, standing up for herself. 'He fancied me up and fancied me down, fancied me up the creek and there he left me.' She tittered. This girl, who so recently couldn't say boo to a goose, had acquired a hard gloss of defiance, like impertinence, from her experiences at the convent.

Alfred said, 'Emily McVeagh has been a friend to most of us here for many years – longer than you have been alive.'

Bright-eyed with anger, Ivy remained silent. Her two supporters – the wives – were also silent.

Rescuing Ivy from the convent, they had promised her a home with one of them.

Ivy was a small dark round girl, rather like a squashed raspberry (Bert's definition), who wore fluffy red jumpers and little short skirts.

Alfred had said to Betsy, 'No, she cannot come and live with us. Don't you do it, Betsy. I'll find myself in bed with her before I know how it happened.'

Alfred was a susceptible man, and Betsy a jealous wife: never had anything so direct been said between them. Mr Redway, perhaps not so old after all, said that Ivy was a girl 'anyone could see, was no better than she ought to be'.

With neither house being ready to take in Ivy, Mary Lane

stepped in. She was alone now in her house; this didn't suit her at all; she would be happy to give Ivy a home. Meeting Alfred out near the pond where the horses bathed, she told him that he needn't worry: Ivy would be married within the year.

'That girl's trouble,' said Alfred, to his old friend Mary. 'She puts my back up. I don't know why.'

Mary knew very well why the men were against Ivy. She desisted from making any of the rude remarks that came to her tongue, and said, 'Alfred, rest yourself. It'll be all right.'

The two Tayler boys, no longer boys, had returned from yet another venture into foreign lands, and at once Tom took a fancy to Ivy.

This conversation took place between father and son. 'Tom,' said Alfred, 'the girl's not twenty-two yet. And you are almost old enough to be her father.'

'Yes, I know, Dad.'

'Are you so set on her?'

'Yes, I am.'

'Then I'm going to ask you to wait a year. You and Michael go off on your trip first.'

'Someone else'll snap her up,' said Tom, grinning.

Which was what Alfred was counting on.

The two wives, having learned that it was their men, as much as 'those nasty old crows', the nuns, who didn't like Ivy, became less belligerent. Even Emily, their embodiment of heartlessness, had been excused by Mary Lane.

Into this atmosphere came Emily, on that chilly afternoon.

Although tousled and reddened, invigorated by the wind, she was in fact pretty tired, having been wrestling with representatives of various Scottish charities all morning.

'Brrrr,' said Emily, briskly, rubbing her hands together. 'I'd forgotten how cold Longerfield can get.'

Emily, who had been on her way to becoming heavy, if not stout, had got thinner nursing Alistair McTaggart and because of tribulations since. She wore a dark-blue costume, with the recently again fashionable fox fur. 'I wonder if that's the fox I shot last spring down near the woods,' said Bert.

'You'll need a cup of tea.' Alfred directed his wife, who was already at the tea tray.

Emily, having taken in the company, understood that the pretty little thing with the baby beside her must be the cause of so much trouble. She said to the girl, smiling, 'Well, I'm Emily Martin-White. Here is the delinquent.'

Ivy offered a crisp little nod in return. Alfred said, 'It's all right, Emily. Mary has explained.'

The wives, who had been holding Emily in their minds for weeks now, as everything they must hate, had only recently relinquished her to her usual place, a formidable elderly woman, who had achieved such miracles of organisation.

'Mary told me that those nuns shut you up in a cell, with nothing to eat but bread and water,' said Emily.

'I gave as good as I got,' said Ivy, haughtily.

'Yes, she did,' said Betsy, excitedly.

'Yes,' enthused Phyllis.

'The nuns were always telling us how sinful we were,' said

Ivy. 'They gave us bad food – and it was because we were sinful; they made us wash all the clothes of the convent in cold water because we were sinful. And I told them that parable, you know, the woman taken in adultery.'

'Indeed, I do,' said Emily, who had been in church every Sunday throughout her childhood.

'Jesus said to the men who were going to stone her, "Let him among you without sin throw the first stone." And before Jesus said that, he bent and wrote something in the dust with his finger. "Have you ever wondered what that could have been, Sister Perpetua?" And she hit me. And I hit her back. That was why they locked me up.'

Emily laughed. 'Good for you.'

'Nothing but bread and cold water, and I was pregnant.' Ivy introduced what was felt to be an unnecessary addition to an overload of accusation.

'It was very wrong,' said Emily.

That word was pursuing her. During the long hours she had been wrestling with the charitable representatives, today Scotland, yesterday Wales, they had repeated how wrong it was that such exemplary schools, like the Martin-White schools, should employ unmarried mothers.

How very much they had enjoyed themselves, Emily recognized, those representatives of public charity, saying, 'It was wrong. It is wrong.'

Wrong, wrong, wrong, agreed Emily now, silently, as one does with words or, for that matter, phrases of tunes, that nag and pester: Now go away. Leave me alone.

Alfred was saying, 'I am so glad you are here, Emily. Because we need to pick your brains. We need your advice, you see.'

Loitering on the lawn, beyond where sat old Mr Redway, were the twins, still called that, the two Tayler boys. Knowing they were going to be wanted at this discussion, they had waited till their father summoned them, which he now did, waving an energetic arm at them as he sat. In bounced Tom, who at once pulled up a chair to sit himself near the disgraced one, who was shining and replete with the attention she had been getting.

The baby squawked; Ivy picked it up, and rocked it in her arms, glancing at Tom, smiling.

She was not altogether sure she wanted to be Alfred's daughter-in-law. On the plus side, everyone knew that Alfred, when Bert died, would be in charge of the farm, possibly an heir. Bert was not long for this world, Ivy had decided. And there was a question of Tom's age. Did she really want to marry an old man? – well, he was certainly attractive, full of the strengths he had acquired on his travels. But not young. Not a young man. There was one of the young farmhands she had noted, had fancied, was keeping in her mind …

Alfred was saying, 'These two boys of mine, well, you've known them since they were born. I don't have to say any more. They've been fighting over there, in more than one war. And then in South America, and in Africa. You tell them … Tom.'

Tom took it up. 'You see, living here, we are so ignorant

about what it's like over there. We aren't anything special, Michael and I, just the education we got here, but if you get into a village, let's say in the Transvaal or in Bolivia, you realize how much we get that others don't. You go into a village, and you are a wonder, what we know. Michael and I set up classes in all kinds of things. You'd be surprised ...

'And if we had a nurse with us, let alone a doctor ...' broke in Michael.

'Yes. And to cut a long story short —'

Alfred took it up: 'We are going to set up a battalion. It's to cut out the recruiters – if a youngster wants to go out of England now the recruiters are waiting for them.'

'The battalion will go, equipped with medics, particularly to the places they can do some good. And that's where we need your help.'

'Oh, you aren't going to ask for my signature,' smiled Emily, who very much liked what she had heard.

'That, too,' said Alfred. 'No, it's your expertise. We have to raise money, you see.'

Emily said: 'I can tell you what Cedric told me – he's our expert. If you can, keep everything under your own control. But that depends on how much money you've got.'

'Not much. But we can raise a good bit around here. No one wants their sons going off to their damned wars.'

'You need Cedric,' said Emily. 'He'll fix you up.'

'To get the young ones out of England, that's the thing,' said Alfred. 'Did you know what a laughing-stock we are? Our bloody class system, our fits of silly public morality ...'

Emily did not think it worthwhile to say again that she was not responsible for the recent scandal.

'They laugh at us,' said Alfred. 'This is a silly, petty, pettifogging little country, and we're so pleased with ourselves because we've kept out of a war. But if you ask me I think a war would do us all the good in the world. We're soft and rotten, like a pear that's gone past its best.'

Here, his sons and his wife began softly clapping at what they had heard too often. They laughed. They were laughing at angry Alfred, who said, 'Oh, laugh, then. But I'm right. If we did have a bit of a war, I mean, not much of one, we wouldn't be so insufferably in the right about everything.'

Emily was not listening to Alfred. The baby, grizzling, was being rocked in those rosy arms. Ivy was smiling, so pretty, in her element, the centre of attention. What a picture, thought Emily, watching how the babe's tiny hands clutched at Ivy's woolly jumper.

So pretty, they are ... and her heart ached. Why did it? There was no reason for it to, surely.

The sight of that young mother and her tiny child was going to make Emily cry again, if she wasn't careful.

'I know I've only just come but if you knew what a day I've had,' excused Emily. 'They wear you out ... And you really must get Cedric on to this, Alfred. It's essential. No, I'm going. I'll just run along.'

General embraces and handshakings.

Emily was out in the wind again, which could be blamed

for her wet eyes and cheeks. She said goodbye to Mr Redway. She left.

Emily did not drop in to Mary's: Daisy was there. Mary and Daisy were not getting on – had they ever? Emily did not want to sit in on a bitter little conversation.

Daisy was saying that Ivy was being rewarded for wrongdoing. It wasn't right. She was going to live in this house and be looked after by Mary. Anyone would think that Ivy had done something wonderful and clever. Emily knew that Daisy did not really think like that: she did when she was with her mother. Mary was not really so condemning, as she was now, of her daughter. 'How can you be so censorious?' and so on.

Emily went to the station and into the waiting-room. A few people waited for the London train.

Emily sat in a corner, and wept.

When Alistair died she had wept, and thought, Of course, one weeps when a friend dies. But it was very different now. She wept because until Alistair had died, and was gone, she had had no idea how much she cared for him. How was that possible? There was something wrong with her. The man had loved her. Now she admitted she had loved him. In the five years they had known each other he had asked her in a hundred different ways to stay with him, had written her delightful little notes and – here was a fact that did not go away – a hundred times could he and she have gone to bed, but for her this had seemed impossible. Why? She did not know. She did not know herself. To sit miserably crying, your heart broken, well, many people have done that. But to sit weeping full of rage, of real fury, at yourself, well, perhaps that is less common.

The station master, between trains to and from London, returned to the waiting-room where a girl stood by the urn that held boiling water, and he and she chatted, and sometimes called out greetings to people in the waiting-room they knew.

Emily, her head in her hands, found a cup of tea sliding towards her and the station master was saying, 'I know who you are. It is hard to see you so low.' And he brought out a flask of something – yes, whisky – and offered it, poised over her teacup. She nodded, thank you. 'My niece was working in your Bristol school,' went on this kindly man. 'It did everything for her. It is a wonderful thing you have done.'

Emily felt redeemed by the tea and the whisky and smiled at her rescuer, who then said that when she heard the train, she must sit right where she was until he came for her. Which he did, taking her out to the platform, his arm around her, until he found the guard, indicated Emily and, with a few whispered words, guaranteed a comfortable journey to London.

Back in Beak Street, she rang Cedric, who at once said, 'So, you are back, Emily.'

And Emily said, 'Cedric, I need to ask you something.'

And he said, 'I know what you are going to ask. I'm psychic – no, it is Fiona. You are going to ask me how much money you have.'

'Yes, that's it. How did Fiona know?'

'Well, armed with my psychic foreknowledge, I looked up your account. You don't have as much as when William left you a tidy little sum, but who is your financial manager? Yes, it is I, Cedric, and you have nearly as much as you did then.'

'Thank you, Cedric. I thought there would be much less.'

'And now Fiona and I have been discussing what you want it for. She says you might be thinking of giving every girl who gets herself into trouble a big sum, enough to catch a husband. I, on the other hand, guessed you might be thinking of starting a refuge – am I right? Well, you have enough money for a really good house, staffed comfortably ...'

'I'm not having any of those ghastly God-bullies,' said Emily.

'Quite right. That's what I told Fiona.'

'I am surprised I am so predictable.'

'Delightfully so, Emily. Like a knight of old, if there is a wrong you are going to right it. Mind you, you don't have enough money to start an empire, like the Martin-White schools, but you could have, let's say, three good refuges. I take it you don't want to go down the road of bishops and debs?'

'Absolutely not. My money, and I'll be sole arbiter.'

'And who could be better?'

'Did your psychic flair tell you about Alfred Tayler and his Good Samaritan battalion?'

'Alfred rang me and asked. If they are going to raise the money themselves, then all he'll need is an accountant: I shall recommend one. Have you decided what to call your refuges?'

Emily told him about Ivy Smith, and how she had quoted the parable of the woman taken in adultery, and had hit the nun who hit her.

'Very good,' said Cedric. 'Well, you can't call it the First Stone, which is what instantly springs to mind. Fiona has already suggested Ruined, after the Hardy poem. The trouble is that finding names, particularly for a dodgy enterprise, always leads one into the temptations of happy ribaldry. Are you crying, Emily?'

'Yes, I can't stop.'

'Have you thought of taking a really good holiday?'

She could not at once speak: since she had known Alistair, she had gone up to see him, stay with him, if she needed to rest.

After a while she said, 'Cedric, I am a very stupid woman and I have only just understood it.'

'Luckily, most of us don't have our stupidities brought home quite so painfully, poor Emily.'

'I shall be very busy starting off the first refuge. I won't have time to think about what a silly woman I am.'

That wasn't exactly true. Since she had seen that girl Ivy, sitting there cuddling the very new infant, the picture hardly left Emily's mind, stabbing her to the heart – which was already overblown with grief.

She, Emily, had had a mother, but she had died. All her life Emily had been saying, 'I didn't really have a mother, she died when I was three.' Emily Flower, her mother, had been considered such a disaster there wasn't even a photograph of her.

Emily Flower had cared only for frivolity and enjoying herself
… Wait a minute – she had had three babies one after another,
and died in childbirth with the third. Did that leave much
room for frivolity and fun? But here was Emily's new thought.
Had it left much time to cuddle and dandle her first baby, little
Emily? Had her mother ever actually held and cuddled and
dandled her, as Emily had seen Ivy do with her new infant?
Did she want to think about it? At least she must decide if she
wanted to think about it. What she did not want was for grief
to rush out of the dark pit it lived in and fasten on her heart,
as had happened with Alistair.

She had to admit that, sitting there in Alfred's house, opposite that girl with her new baby, smiling, defiant, she, Emily,
had wanted to kill her. Yes. Why had she? She had certainly
never felt anything like that with Fiona and her infants.

Cedric said, 'You shouldn't worry too much about Ivy
Smith. If there was ever a girl who could look after herself …'

'She didn't do too well looking after herself with us, did
she?'

'True. She nearly split the Martin-White Foundation down
the middle. But surely the fault is with our delightful British
public, not with her.'

'Probably.'

'Why don't you come and see me in the morning and we
will arrange absolutely everything? I don't mind if you cry.
Cry as much as you like.'

ALFRED TAYLER was a very old man when he died. He came from a long-lived family.

EMILY MCVEAGH saw some boys tormenting a dog and went to remonstrate. They turned on her. It was believed that her shock at this was more the reason for her heart-attack than the blow she received on her head. She was seventy-three years old. Hundreds of people came to her funeral.

Explanation

You can be with old people, even those getting on a bit, and never suspect that whole continents of experience are there, just behind those ordinary faces. Best to be old yourself to understand, if not one of those percipient children made sensitive by having to learn watchfulness, knowing that a glance, a tiny gesture may mean warnings or rewards. Two old people may exchange a look where tears are implicit, or say, 'Do you remember …' signposts to something worth remembering for thirty years. Even a tone of voice, a warmth, or irritation, can mark a ten-year love affair, or an enmity. Writing about parents, even alert offspring or children may miss gold. 'Oh, yes, that was when I was living in Doncaster that summer with Mavis.'

'You were *what?* You never mentioned that.'

Writing about my father's imagined life, my mother's, I have relied not only on traits of character that may be extrapolated, or extended, but on tones of voice, sighs, wistful looks, signs as slight as those used by skilful trackers.

More than once did my father say, with a laugh, talking

about some girl in his youth, 'But I liked her mother even more.' From there came Alfred's intimacy with Mary Lane.

Bert was his childhood friend, a young man's mate. They had good times together in boys' pastimes and when Bert went with my father to the races, 'Oh, I did so love the horses,' said my father. Meaning the animals themselves. 'Bert and I went up to Doncaster when we could. But I was on my guard – I could easily be taken over by it all – those horses thundering down the straight with the sun on their hides, the smell of them, the slippery run of your hand on a rump. But Bert wasn't so cautious, not in that or in anything. I used to have to watch for Bert. He didn't care enough about himself.'

Once in Banket, in Rhodesia, for no reason I can remember, there was a Danish woman visiting. She was a large, laughing, ruddy-faced woman and I remember to this day sitting as a small girl on her lap, in her arms, thinking, She likes me, she likes me better than my mother does. And my father most certainly did like her. From that afternoon so long ago came Betsy, Alfred's wife: I enjoyed giving him someone warm and loving.

William, Emily McVeagh's husband, came from the little picture of my mother's great love that lived on her dressing-table. But, strange, it was a cutting from a newspaper in that leather frame, not a portrait from a studio or a friendly snap. Yet she talked as if she and he were to be married. It was a sensitive, cautious face, the sort of face you'd cast in a film as the lover too shy to speak his love, or whose first love died young, leaving him grieving and for ever unable to love another. Even as a child I would look at that face and think, Well, you wouldn't have had much fun with that one. Meaning fun, the kind of good times my father talked about in London before the war.

Daisy was my mother's great friend all her life until, after many decades of writing England to Africa, Southern Rhodesia to London, they met again and I think did not find much in common. Daisy in life did not marry, but she was of the generation that did not find husbands: they were killed in the war, the war to end all wars.

Both Emily and Alfred, when young, knew how to make the most of London. They went to the theatre – my father loved the music hall; my mother enjoyed concerts; they had supper at the Trocadero, and the Café Royal. What energy they had, both of them. Cricket, tennis, hockey, picnics, parties, dances.

Cedric and Fiona, the young couple who liked Emily, were suggested by the couples, younger than she was, who befriended my mother. She always had admirers, younger, sometimes much richer, who liked her energy, her humour, her flair, her impetuous way with life. She also had male admirers. The one place in my mother's imagined life where I have taken serious liberties is her friendship with Alistair. He loved her but she did not know it, or didn't want to know it. This was suggested by the time after my father's death when my brother and I tried to persuade her to marry again.

It was partly selfish: we made no excuses about wanting that formidable energy directed away from us. But there was also concern for her. She had had that long bad time, nursing

– years of it – with nothing in her life but a very sick man, her husband, who needed her every minute. Now there were men who wanted to marry her, sensible, quite impressive men, one a bank manager – surely up her street – another a well-off farmer. She could at last stop worrying about money, have decent holidays, companionship. But our attempts were met not only without enthusiasm but as if what we were suggesting was out of the question. But why? demanded my brother. Why not? I pressed and persuaded. It was her incomprehension that silenced us. That we should suggest such an impossible, inconceivable thing! How could we? 'How could I marry anyone but your father? And besides, I must devote myself to my children.' Who were grown-up, with lives well away from her.

We actually discussed it, my brother and I, though chat about the emotions was not really our habit. 'But why not one of them?' demanded my brother. 'So-and-so – he's a perfectly decent chap, isn't he? What is the matter with Derek, then, or Charles? I think he loves her, you know,' said Harry, blushing at this inordinate use of language. 'Why shouldn't she have something nice happen to her at last?' But no. Anyone would think we were suggesting she should mate with King Kong.

'You know,' my brother tried again, in a fever of embarrassment, 'you know, Mother, I think Charles is really keen on you.'

'You really are so funny, you two,' said my mother, briskly.

From *The London Encyclopaedia*,
edited by Ben Weinreb and Christopher Hibbert, 1983

Royal Free Hospital, Pond Street, Hampstead, NW3

Founded by William Marsden, a young surgeon who was inspired with the idea of free admissions to hospitals when he found a young woman dying on the steps of ST ANDREW'S CHURCH in HOLBORN and was unable to get admission for her at any of the London hospitals which all then demanded letters of recommendation from a subscriber. On 14 February 1828, Marsden met members of the CORDWAINERS' COMPANY at the Gray's Inn Coffee House where they resolved to found the first hospital to admit patients without payment or a subscriber's letter. The hospital opened on 17 April 1828 under the patronage of King George IV and with the Duke of Gloucester as its first President. It has continued to receive royal patronage ever since. The original site was a small rented house at No.16 Greville Street, HATTON GARDEN, with only a few beds. The hospital, though familiarly called 'The Free Hospital', was officially known as the London General Institution for the Gratuitous Care of Malignant Diseases. In 1837, when Queen Victoria became Patron, she asked that it should henceforth be known as the Royal Free Hospital. In the first year 926 patients were treated. In the second year the hospital dealt with 1,551 cases. In 1832 over 700 cholera patients were treated. A matron and nurse were employed while the epidemic lasted. In 1839 another house was acquired and the number of beds rose from 30 to 72.

With rapidly growing public support, a larger building was necessary, and in 1843 the hospital moved to a site in GRAY'S INN ROAD which had formerly been the barracks of the Light Horse Volunteers. The lease was purchased on 31 August 1843. The hospital extended its facilities on the new site, the Sussex Wing being opened in 1856 in memory of the Duke of Sussex. In 1877 the teaching of students began, and thus the hospital became one of the first of the London undergraduate teaching hospitals. The Victoria Wing with an out-patient department was added in 1878; and the Alexandra Building was opened by the Prince of Wales in 1895. The numerous benefactors included Lord Riddell, Sir Albert Levy, Free-masons, and several of the CITY LIVERY COMPANIES. Apart from the pioneer principle of its inception, the Royal Free took a leading part in two other important aspects of hospital work, the introduction of women medical students in 1877 and of a Lady Almoner in 1895.

The admission of women to study medicine was the most momentous step in the history of the hospital and the provision of clinical facilities for women students marked the triumphant climax of a struggle for recognition that had been going on for some years by a small group of brave and determined women led by Elizabeth Garrett Anderson and Sophia Jex-Blake. Until 1894 all the medical members of the consultant and resident staff were men, but in that year Miss L.B. Aldrich-Blake was appointed as honorary anaesthetist. In the following year she obtained the MS London, the first woman to secure this qualification, and she subsequently became a distinguished surgeon on the hospital staff. In 1901 women were accepted as resident medical officers.

In 1921 it became the first hospital in England to have an obstetrics and gynaecology unit. In 1926–30 the Eastman Dental Hospital was built to the designs of Burnet, Tait and Lorne. The Royal Free suffered severe damage in the Second World War, with considerable loss of beds.

In 1948, with the inception of the National Health Service, the Royal Free Hospital became the centre of a group of hospitals which included the HAMPSTEAD GENERAL HOSPITAL, the ELIZABETH GARRETT ANDERSON HOSPITAL, the London Fever Hospital (Liverpool Road), the North West Fever Hospital (Lawn Road) and subsequently also New End and Coppetts Wood Hospitals. The ELIZABETH GARRETT ANDERSON HOSPITAL later separated from the group while the HAMPSTEAD GENERAL, North West Fever and London Fever Hospitals were incorporated with the parent hospital and its medical school in the new Royal Free Hospital, which was built on its present site to the designs of Watkins, Gray, Woodgate International. The first patient was admitted in October 1974; the hospital was in full use by March 1975; and was officially opened by the Queen on 15 November 1978.

There are now 1,070 beds comprising 852 in the new building, 144 at New End Hospital (New End, NW3) and 74 at Coppetts Wood Hospital (Coppetts Road, MUSWELL HILL, N10).

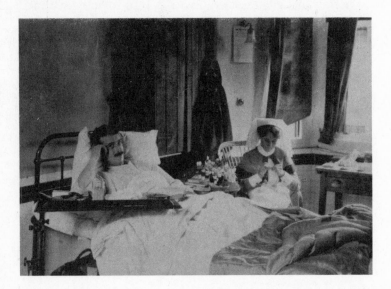

PART TWO

Alfred and Emily; Two Lives

And dimly she realised one of the great laws of the human soul: that when the emotional soul receives a wounding shock, which does not kill the body, the soul seems to recover as the body recovers. But this is only appearance. It is, really, only the mechanism of re-assumed habit. Slowly, slowly the wound to the soul begins to make itself felt, like a bruise which only slowly deepens its terrible ache, till it fills all the psyche. And when we think we have recovered and forgotten, it is then that the terrible after-effects have to be encountered at their worst.

D. H. LAWRENCE, *Lady Chatterley's Lover*

I have written about my father in various ways; in pieces long and short, and in novels. He comes out clearly, unambiguous, all himself. One may write a life in five volumes, or in a sentence. How about this? Alfred Tayler, a vigorous and healthy man, was wounded badly in the First World War, tried to live as if he were not incapacitated, illnesses defeated him, and at the end of a shortened life he was begging, 'You put a sick old dog out of its misery, why not me?'

This sentence ignores impressive things. He would ride, in Kermanshah, Persia, to his work at the bank. I've seen him go down a rough mine shaft in a bucket, his wooden leg sticking out and banging against the rocky sides. He ran, or hobbled, in fathers' races at my brother's school. He climbed a difficult tree to a tree-house made by my brother and me. He would go stomping through the bush, more than once taking a fall, or clamber over the great clods in a ploughed field.

The contraption that enabled him to do all this was called by him 'my wooden leg', and it lived, in duplicate, leaning against a wall in the parental bedroom. Recently Burroughs and Wellcome had an exhibition of their products past and present in the British Museum and there in a glass case, a museum piece, I saw my father's wooden leg. It consisted of a bucket shape in wood, into which the poor wasted stump was put, on a metal leg and foot, and heavy straps that held the device in place. The stump was fitted with stump socks, in knitted wool, up to ten of them, according to the weather and the condition of the stump. If the weather was hot, the socks were itchy and uncomfortable. When my father got diabetes and lost weight, he filled the well with layers of wool. The War Office supplied the wooden leg, and replacements when it wore out. On to the foot went ordinary socks and a shoe. The knee was flexible, in metal. This contraption in no way resembled the artificial legs of now, which are light and clever and can do everything.

That sentence resumé does not mention the diabetes, which, when they first found insulin, was managed with none of the subtlety they use now.

Reading what I wrote about my father, listening in my mind's ear to things he said, one thing stands out. Medicine generally has evolved so that probably most people now would not recognize its clumsiness at the time my father was wounded. He said that his mind was full of horrors as he lay in hospital: 'Dreadful things, horrible, awful. I would wake up screaming.' My mother, nursing him, confirmed. 'I was afraid to sleep.'

This sounds like post-traumatic stress disorder, long before the condition was described, but surely not the idea. 'Shell shock' has in its syllables the sense of trauma. The doctor, called by my father 'that nice doctor chap', suggested that my father was lucky to have avoided shell shock.

There are pills for it today, surely, and for what sounds to me like a major depression: 'I was inside a dark cloud. It clung to me. You see, the men who were killed and wounded, the men in my company, oh, they were such fine chaps. I couldn't stop thinking of them. There was such a weight on my heart. My heart felt like a big cold stone ...'

People who have experienced grief will testify that it is felt in the heart, like a weight of cold pain.

But no mention was made of medicines. Bromide, was it? If so, it didn't seem to do much for him.

If he had post-traumatic stress disorder or very bad depression these days, there would be miraculous pills, dulling it all.

And now, looking back at that life, it is evident to me that my father, during the dreadful slow end of it, was depressed. Now the grim and ghastly depressions of old people are common knowledge. He would be medicated out of the worst of it. But no one then suggested that my father was ill with bipolar or any other depression and needed serious medicines.

My father slept badly for all his life, what there was of it; he dreamed of his old comrades, and grieved for them. Yes, the pain of grief does soften and go, but at the breakfast table he might say to my mother, 'I was dreaming of Tommy again,' or Johnny or Bob. 'There he was, telling me a joke about something.' Quite right! Dead soldiers simply should not be angry ghosts displaying their wretched wounds. He was a great joker, obviously, Tommy or Johnny or Bob, and I think the Bairnsfather cartoons, much relished in our house, were responsible for that. Old Bill, the archetypical British Tommy, didn't go in for grief or repining, whether up to his waist in dead water in a shell hole, or trying to hide from the shells under a bright moon. 'The same dear old moon is looking down on *him*,' was the caption of one cartoon: a girl in England with her hair floating looks at the moon out of her bedroom window, and meanwhile her lover is cowering from it under shell-fire. 'The same dear old moon is looking down on ...' became a bit of a catchphrase for us, the children included.

Thus. It is bright moonlight, we stand on the hill and down there the great mealie field is rippling in the moonrays, just green, just not green. It is possible to see there are people too because parts of the field are gently agitated. 'Thieves,' says my father, pleased because of the predictability of it all. 'What's the sense,' he enquires of the night, the universe, 'to go stripping cobs under a bright moon?'

'While the same dear old moon is looking down on us,' says my mother.

Or, my brother off at boarding school, and she is mourning because of his absence: 'The same dear old moon ...'

'Oh, come off it, old girl,' says my father, bruised by the sentimentality she enjoys.

She had never understood why her higher flights embarrassed him. We, the children, were appalled by them. But some kinds of sentimentality have in them an antidote. She was moved, her voice was rich with tears. She felt it, all right. But isn't sentimentality intolerable because it is false feeling? My mother was capable of weeping because of Oates going out into the snow – 'I may be some time' – or the Last Post coming from the noisy radio that was so hard to keep steady on a wavelength. Yet when something terrible had to be done, like shooting an ill dog or drowning kittens, she did it, lips tight, face hard. She complained that my father had a cold heart.

When she was ill, shortly after reaching the farm, she was intolerably sentimental, and this leads me straight into the hardest part of what I am trying to understand.

Nothing that she ever told, or was said about her, or one could deduce of her in that amazing girlhood, so busy, so full of achievement, or of her nursing years, about which we had the best of witnesses, my father himself, or the years in Persia, so enjoyable and so social, nothing, anywhere, in all this matches up with what my mother became.

Nothing fits, as if she were not one woman but several.

As a child I was desperately sorry for my mother, even when I was planning to run away (how? in the bush? where to?). I was sorry for her because she was hardly silent about her sufferings. And that is where we begin with the question, when was Emily McVeagh ever self-pitying, complaining, sorry for herself? I don't think it was in her. And yet it must have been, the self-pitying tears welled up when she was sick with 'a heart-attack' and took to her bed.

Now let's look at this superbly healthy, energetic woman, who has brought two little children, five and three, all the way

from Tehran to London, by ship to Cape Town, to Beira, by
train to Salisbury, who helped her invalid husband choose a
farm in uncharted, unworked wilderness, got the house built,
from materials she had never seen and knew nothing about,
got the house furnished, as was the way with 'the settlers',
making curtains from dyed flour sacks, cupboards and tables
from paraffin boxes, making everything herself – and then she
and her husband got malaria, twice. Is there a clue there
perhaps? Very debilitating, is malaria. And then, in that house,
made of mud and grass, matching it with what she thought
she was coming to, stuck there, and she knew it, she took to
her bed with a heart-attack.

This was a nurse. She had nursed for years in one of the
world's great hospitals. She had nursed the wounded of a
world war, and now it is easy to see she was in a state of dreadful anxiety, she was full of panic, she could look ahead and see
she was trapped, with no way out. A heart-attack. So she said.
She lay on her bed while my father coped with clearing bush,
buying machinery, employing labour – about which he knew
nothing at all – looking after the two little children, with the
aid of a drunken widow calling herself a housekeeper. It was
not like her, my mother. This was simply not what she was.
She called her little children to her, and she said, 'Poor
Mummy, poor, poor Mummy.'

To this day I can feel the outrage I felt then. I was outraged,
in a rage, furious, and of course desperately sorry for her. Was
she ill? She was, if not with a heart-attack. She was ill, all right.
And not herself. That was the point. And what were we sup-

posed to do? Kiss her? Give her a good hug? But she did not only demand our pity with tears to match hers. That was not all she did.

The man who ran a sawmill, four miles off, admired her, and had made her a contraption to swing into place over her bed so she could read. He was one of the people I remember who thought my mother a marvel. To this reading device she summoned us and gave us our first lessons. I don't remember what they were. I was too hot and angry. 'You must look after your little brother,' said my mother, in a voice sick with senti-ment. But looking after my little brother had been my burden, my task, my responsibility, my pride always. Why, suddenly, did she insist on it now?

She was in bed, so she would tell us later, for a year, but it was not as long. Was it the drunken housekeeper who made it essential for her to get out of bed? Or was it the drunken housekeeper's out-of-control twelve-year-old son, who beat up cats and dogs and bullied us?

She got up, and what that must have cost her I cannot begin to imagine. She was saying goodbye to everything she had expected for her life in this colony, which must have been something like Happy Valley in Kenya. (But if she had experi-enced Happy Valley she would have been disgusted by it.) In the trunk behind the Liberty curtain lay the evening dresses, the gloves, the feathers, the hats. In a purse put away some-where the visiting cards she had made especially for this life.

But the piano stood in the living-room, whose windows were shaped like portholes, looking out over that bush, and she played. She played, well, everything – but I was brought up knowing that the right accompaniment to Chopin and Beethoven was the thudding of native drums.

Now I look back and know that she had a bad breakdown, of everything she had been and was. That woman whimpering in her sickbed, 'Pity me, pity', it was not her.

But I have got ahead of myself, or beside myself. It is because of the impossibility of making sense of Time in its boundaries. Known boundaries and that is the point. I was having my fifth birthday on a German ship in the Atlantic, and when I was seven, was sent to the convent. Two years and perhaps a bit more. Into that time have to be fitted the following. The family went by slow train to Salisbury, where the children were left in a guesthouse, 'Lilfordia', while my parents went to look for a farm. Not in a nice, speedy car, but in a pony and trap. The farm found, we children and the trunks followed in a covered wagon, of the kind we see in films.

There being no house on our farm, the family were lodging with the Whiteheads, small-mine owners, while the house was being built and the lands marked out from the bush. Well, it need not take long to throw up mud walls and a thatched roof. And malaria – twice, for all of us.

And now I have to fit in Biddy O'Halloran, who was supposed to be aiding my mother with her two little children. An au pair, she would be now. For both parents this girl was trouble and annoyance. The watching Fates must have been getting a good laugh out of the situation. Biddy was a modern girl, an entity much defended, or attacked, in those days. She smoked, had her hair in a shingle and wore lipstick, which my mother was doing herself very soon, but meanwhile she thought Biddy shameless. The trouble was that my parents were in Persia in the feverish post-war years. They missed the jazz, the Charleston, girls cutting off their hair with the *élan* with which girls burned their bras later. Dresses were at knee-length – or mini-length. Girls swore and drank, demanded the freedom to be like men.

Biddy O'Halloran appalled my father, too. Young men kept turning up, because of the new girl in the district. Many wanted wives, wanted them badly. No one could make a success of farming if he had no wife. My father hit one youth who asked for Biddy. 'I think you must mean Miss O'Halloran?' he demanded. 'But I am *in loco parentis*. I am responsible for her.' Were there darker currents here? Did my father 'like' Biddy – as we children would primly put it? Was my mother jealous of Biddy? Emily Tayler's years in Persia had been all pleasure to the point that my father protested, 'I had no idea I was marrying a social butterfly.' In England, not much fun, but there was the boat. She and the captain got on famously. My father was sick in his berth. No one was ever better fitted for a sea voyage than my mother: she adored deck games and dances, and dressing up – all of it – and the German captain clearly admired her. The belle of the ball she must have been, with that trunk full of delicious frocks, but then there were the farm and impertinent Biddy, and everything went wrong, and very fast.

I owe to Biddy a memory that is one of the most important I have.

On the mine, the children – my brother, me and the White-heads – slept in a large hut. Four beds, each under a long white shroud, the mosquito net. The floor was mud with coconut matting. The roof was thatch.

Biddy comes into the hut with a candle and she stands looking about, wondering where to set it down. Beside my bed a little night-table – a paraffin box painted. She sets down the candlestick on this, and the flame of the candle is half an inch from the mosquito net, which would flare up like a lit match, or a firework, if it caught. My mother enters just behind Biddy. She sees what Biddy has done. Slowly, so as not to set up a current of fast air that might encourage the flame to reach for the net, she comes over, gently lifts the candlestick and takes it to set down on a table far from danger. She is white, she is clutching her throat. When she sits, or collapses, into a chair, she is trembling. If that flame had caught the net – mine – it would have flared, and set off the other three. One may not imagine anything more attractive to fire than a mosquito net, an airy pillar of white cotton. If the nets had flared, so would the thatch over our heads, and the tempestuously burning hut would have set off the whole group of thatched huts.

'What are you doing?' my mother asks Biddy, and her voice is cracked and whispery. Her mind is full of roaring flames, screaming children, the hut falling on us, the screams from the other huts …

What she is imagining is reaching me: I am already aware of and wary of fire. I begin to cry.

'What is wrong?' asks Biddy, quickly. She might just as well have twiddled a frond of her hair with a much-ringed finger, or sung a phrase or two of some winsome Irish folk tune. That there is something wrong my mother's voice told her, not to mention my crying. 'But nothing happened,' she says pertly, at last. Nothing has.

But in my mother's imagination everything was happening. She sat staring at Biddy and it is this that will never leave my mind. She is uncomprehending, bewildered. Her lips are white. Between the clever, foresightful people of this world and the ones without imagination there is a gulf into which perhaps we will all fall one day. My mother can't believe that Biddy – or anyone – could do what she did.

'I think I'll go to bed,' says Biddy, and goes off to her hut. My mother sits quite still, then she puts her face into her hands, which are shaking, and she weeps, dry, helpless sobs. 'Oh, my God, oh, my God.'

Biddy was not exactly clever with children. She told my brother that if he didn't keep his mouth shut grasshoppers would jump in and eat up his stomach. She told me a tree would grow out of me like *Jack and the Beanstalk*. My brother screamed and had nightmares. I didn't believe in the tree but I early attained that admirable balance of small children. I was capable of believing and not believing at the same time. No tree – no, but what fun if there was …

Biddy left and my mother took to her bed. Biddy, later in Ireland, married a younger son and was to be seen in society columns. It is around then that I put the drunken house-keeper and her pathetic son, who now it is so easy to see as the victim of a marital breakdown. My mother sent for the gov-ernment correspondence course. Every week the lessons arrived by train. Then I was sent for a term to a kindly place full of pleasant people. It seemed years I was there. Then I was put into a family near to Avondale Junior School, but they were cruel and stupid people. Much time passed there. Then they sent me to the convent school. Only two years had passed, and even now I can't make it all fit. So many people, events, dramas, the malaria, watching the house-building. I learned to read off a cigarette packet. 'Look, I can read.' And then I was at the convent. Children should not be sent away from home aged seven. It does them no good at all.

But while I can remember vividly the difficult things, the drunk woman who shared my bedroom, my mother lying for ever in bed, I remember better a delight of my childhood that began about the time my mother got out of bed.

She told us stories. 'More ... More, please go on ... more, please.' She made whole epics out of the mice in the store-room, the rats, the cats, the dogs, the chickens in the fowl run. A central feature of these tales was the tower of eggs in the storeroom, coveted by the mice and by the rats, who most ingeniously knew how to roll eggs free to smash and become available to them.

What a wonderful storyteller she was. She read to us too, and they were wonderful tales, but nothing would compare with her stories.

It is 1924, and two little people stand on the quay, watching how their luggage is being swung, piece after piece, up and over the ship's side. My mother was counting the pieces: she could never believe others were as efficient as herself. 'Wanted on Voyage'. 'Not Wanted on Voyage'. They were about to sail off into the future, with as little understanding of the life they would lead as the first voyagers for Jamestown, or on the *Mayflower* later, on the east coast of America.

In those trunks and cases was everything for their imagined life. My father's had accoutrements and clothes for cricket: he had scarcely played in Persia, but now he was going to a British colony and cricket there must be. A trunk held riding things. Not for hunting in the English manner – foxes and stags – but what a gentleman who always rode rather than walked would need. A long wooden case held his wooden legs. My mother's imagined life held more variety. First, the trunk with the dozen or so dark-red leather volumes of music scores – Liszt, Beethoven, Chopin, Grieg, all of them – and, too, sheets of popular music, music-hall songs and ballads sung when she was a girl around an Edwardian piano. A trunk, 'Wanted on Voyage', of evening frocks, scarves, gloves, hats, boas, bags, silvery stockings, brocaded shoes.

This former nurse took her earlier life with her: catheters, enemas, douches, stethoscopes, measuring glasses. These were in the bottom half of a trunk that had on its top layer the

Mason's equipment about which my father was so blisteringly sarcastic. Why did he take these things to Africa?

There was another box, or case, full of things for teaching children, crayons and chalks, and books. So this plenitude, the great heavenly provision, was there on the farm from the very start.

Where may one start?

A Child's Garden of Verses, Stevenson.
The House at Pooh Corner, all of A. A. Milne.

Children's annuals and collections. Readers of all kinds.

These were what she took with her. On the farm she ordered from England books for us. This meant laying out on the dining-table the Croxley writing-paper, pens, ink, and she wrote carefully long lists of books. They were addressed to London bookstores, stamped, and the envelope was taken by the boy on his bicycle to the station where it was handed in at the post office. Banket station, like a score or more of the stations in Rhodesia, consisted of, most important, the post office, a grocery for whites, another for blacks, a butcher, a 'hotel' – a dining-room off a brick veranda, gauzed for flies, and in it half a dozen tables and a few chairs. There were two bedrooms. There was the station building too. A real bar, but for whites only. The authorities, mindful of what had happened to the peoples of America when alcohol struck them, would not allow the locals to drink anything but their own 'kaffir beer'. Quite soon this would become a political issue.

The letter was carried by train to Salisbury, taken to the post office there, and put on a train to Beira or to Cape Town. A ship took the precious letter to London, England. The letter was read, big brown-paper parcels were made up, tied with thick string, and they were on the ship to Cape Town and Beira. Then the reverse journey: the train to Salisbury and that post office, the train to Banket, where the parcels waited in the station office till the 'boy', or sometimes my mother, would come to collect them. And then the joy of those parcels, spread out on the dining-table, on the spare bed in my room. When I came from school for holidays the parcels would be waiting for me: my mother did not unpack them. My brother? He was never interested.

There was a *Children's Newspaper*, made in London, with items from the general news rewritten for children, poems, stories, by Walter de la Mare and Eleanor Farjeon, a wonderful periodical – hours of enjoyment with each issue. This was the time when they were excavating in Egypt and in Ur – Iraq. They made magazines out of the stories of the finds, and photographs of the treasures. My mother ordered these, and the rooms under the thatch were illuminated for days with the pictures of Tutankhamun and Nefertiti, and the hoard of his possessions, with the golden artefacts from Ur.

Alice in Wonderland
The Secret Garden
The Wind in the Willows

Struwwelpeter

Children's Tales from Homer

Greek Myths for Children

The Sagas for Children

Black Beauty

Biffel a Trex Ox – a South African story about an ox
  working through the *rinderpest* epidemic. Oh, the
  tears, the sorrow.

Jock of the Bushveld

Kim

The Just So Stories

The Jungle Tales

The Scarlet Pimpernel

Huckleberry Finn

Peter Pan

A Life of Rhodes

A Life of Florence Nightingale

A Life of Wilberforce

Walter de la Mare's *The Three Royal Monkeys* and his
  Poems

Longfellow

Beatrix Potter's *Tales*

Uncle Remus

The Young Visiters, by Daisy Ashford

Little Black Sambo but since this hero did not resemble
  in any way the black people I was surrounded by, not
  in face, or in how he spoke or how he dressed, I was

an adult before I understood that the golliwog-like creature was meant to be human. Caricature should not be too far from its subject.

There were children's books from America, and some specifically for girls:

Louisa May Alcott, *Little Women, Good Wives, Little Men*
L. M. Montgomery, *Anne of Green Gables, Anne of Avonlea, Anne's House of Dreams*
Eleanor Hodgman, the *Pollyanna* books
Gene Stratton Porter, *Girl of the Limberlost, Laddie, The Keeper*
Harriet Beecher Stowe, *Uncle Tom's Cabin*
Susan Coolidge, *What Katy Did*, and other Katy stories

And the American writers who did not write specifically for children, of whom the best was Ernest Thompson Seton. He wrote about animals, and I had several by him, the best and most memorable being *Lobo, A Wolf*, but there were others about prairie dogs, a bear, a stag, a silver fox.

Jack London, *The Call of the Wild, White Fang, People of the Abyss, The Sea Wolf*
The Poems of Tennyson
The Legend of Arthur and the Round Table
Hans Christian Andersen

Tales of the Brothers Grimm
Charles Kingsley, *The Water Babies*

Improbably, a wonderful book of fairy tales from Brazil, whose wildly romantic illustrations intoxicated me.

Nathaniel Hawthorne, *Sleepy Hollow*
John Bunyan, *Pilgrim's Progress*

In the bookcase made of black-lacquered paraffin boxes, were all of Dickens, Kipling in his limp red-leather covers, all of Walter Scott, Ruskin; and novels popular in 1924: for instance, *Forest Lovers* – by Maurice Hewlett – and a now forgotten novel by H. G. Wells, *Joan and Peter,* which much influenced my parents' generation, all about education.

So this stream of books for children came pouring through our house and sometimes out again, for my mother complained, but was pleased about it, that people saw her as a kind of library. My father joined a book club in England for books about the Great War in Europe. Books by generals, the memoirs of, the lives of, the war years of … books of all kinds but very few – they came later – by women. A book related the adventures of a woman fighting in Russia who pretended to be a man, and got away with it till the war ended. A book about two women nursing the Serbian wounded. A book about VADs – Voluntary Aid Workers – in France.

These war books continued a theme: that there are two

kinds of old soldier, those who cannot stop talking about their war, and those who shut up and never say a word. If this last sounds improbable, I met a man in the United States whose business it was (and still is) to accompany soldiers from the Second World War back to the scenes of their trial. There he discovered an amazing thing. The wives of those men went with them, and it turned out they had never heard a word of what their men had been through: they heard it all, for the first time, actually standing with their men in the places where it had been.

My father was of the first kind. Even as a child I knew his obsessive talking about the Trenches was a way of ridding himself of the horrors. So I had the full force of the Trenches, tanks, star-shells, shrapnel, howitzers – the lot – through my childhood, and felt as if the black cloud he talked about was there, pressing down on me. I remember crouching in the bush, my hands tight over my ears: 'I won't, I will not. Stop. I won't listen.' My mother's voice? I could have listened, but it was all too much. The fate of parents who most terribly need their offspring to listen, to 'take in' something of their own substance, is often to be thwarted. My father's need was, as it were, legitimate. The Trenches, yes, I had to accept that. But my mother also needed a listener, and to her needs I tried to be oblivious. Later, much later, did I see that my mother's wartime ordeals were ravag-ing her from within just as my father's Trenches were eating away at him.

For the years of the war, my mother nursed the men wounded in the Trenches. The wounded who could be saved went to local dressing stations and then were put on trains to London or other British cities. After the great battles, all the London hospitals were on alert for the influx of men, who would arrive in ambulances, lorries, even carts, to be put along the corridors and in any space available. 'We had no room, you see,' she would mourn. 'There was no space for them. We didn't have enough beds. They were so young, you see, so dreadfully young, those poor boys. They were dying. They were sometimes dead when they arrived. We did what we could. We would make wards for them out of the corridors. But they died, you see, and often we could do nothing. That was the awful thing. Sometimes there was nothing we could do. The medicines held out, though once or twice it was a close call. I remember once we ran out of morphine and that was so terrible. It was so terrible, do you see ...'

And it went on, the awfulness, one year and into the next, and then another year. Sister McVeagh and her gallant band of nurses. 'We were sometimes so tired you'd see a nurse keel over, asleep, as she was attending to a patient.' And it all went on. She nursed her husband, Alfred Tayler, who nearly died, in the operation of taking his leg off, and it all went on, and on, and on. 'That was it, do you see? It never seemed to end. And we'd finish doing our best after one battle, like Passchendaele, and then there was another battle and they came pouring in again. I can hear them call out now, 'Nurse, Nurse.' I can hear them. 'Oh, the pain, Nurse, oh, Nurse, the pain.' And my mother, who I maintain could have been an actress, made the sounds of the poor boys calling out for morphine painful, years and years later. 'And the worst, you see, the worst was when they were calling for their mothers. They were just boys, that's all. I remember one little lad, he was sixteen, he had pretended to be eighteen, but he was just … He died calling for his mother, and I …' and Sister McVeagh, all those years later, wept, remembering how she had pretended to be his mother. '"Yes, I'm here," I said. Oh, and when I think of it …'

Well, she did think of it, a great deal, and at times two streams of war horrors went on together, my mother's 'Oh, the poor boys' like a descant to the Trenches.

So there was this load of suffering deep inside my mother, as there was inside my father, and please don't tell me that this kind of pain, borne for years, doesn't take its dreadful toll.

It took me years – and years – and years – to see it: my mother had no visible scars, no wounds, but she was as much a victim of the war as my poor father.

Thinking about those years, it is easy to feel them now like parallel streams of experiences: the books, the talk of war, the reminiscences, then, the illnesses, physical and mental. Stronger than all of these, the bush, being in it. A pity one cannot say to a child, an adolescent, who feels as if she were as circumscribed as a girl living in suburbs far from any fun, 'Just look at yourself. Well, look. You have at your fingers' ends the world's literature for children. You have the last war distilled into books, let alone running in the living talk of your parents. You listen to the BBC, and your parents talk about European politics. And when you walk out of your bedroom door you as likely as not encounter a porcupine out for its evening stroll, or a kudu, or any one of the big snakes. Look up and a hundred hawks are hanging there, above your head. How many children in the world ...' etc.

Ten years after their arrival in Banket – that is, shortly before my father was diagnosed with diabetes, and the slow, then faster descent into serious illness and death had begun – affairs on the farm were bad. We were in the doldrums, idling in a backwater. Nothing went right, and already it was 'But when we get back to England, then ...'

What was to blame?

How attractive are the tidy conclusions of hindsight! How satisfying the *of course* of the back-looking perspective. *Of course* if you do this, then that will happen ...

Now it is so easy to see that nothing could go right.

It was entirely their fault, but how could they have seen it? First, you have to be able to see yourselves in relation to circumstances, see the family and that house, wrapped in myth and the perspectives of 'If only ...' or 'If we had known ...'

My parents, on leave from Persia, were at the Empire Exhibition, and the Southern Rhodesian stall had great mealie cobs, and the invitation: 'Get rich on maize.' Do you mean to say those idiots believed a slogan on a stall at an exhibition? But many idiots did, and went out and grew maize and got rich. During the war, fortunes had been made growing maize, bought by governments to feed soldiers and animals.

But the people who had done this were already switching to tobacco where they would do very well indeed.

But my father wasn't interested in getting rich. He wanted to make enough money to return to England and fulfil his dream to buy a farm in Essex or Suffolk or Norfolk and be an English farmer. But my mother was dreaming of something different. Farming in Rhodesia would be a continuation of her hectic life in Persia, all parties and fun. And nowhere more than here do I have difficulty in trying to match up with the mother I knew, always ill, long-suffering, dutiful, attending the needs of others like an Edwardian lady, with the 'social butterfly'.

The government of Southern Rhodesia invited ex-servicemen to come out, be given land and farm on loans from the Land Bank. The object of this was plainly stated and it never occurred then to anyone except, of course, the blacks who had been defeated in war, to question the sense of it: settling the whites from England was, specifically, to establish white civilization, and uplift the blacks. The Romans thought like this; so has every empire anywhere at any time. My parents believed in empire and its benefits.

So what was to prevent them being exactly like all their neighbours and getting rich on tobacco?

It was themselves, their nature.

First, the farm was too small to achieve anything in the way of serious profit. It was a mixed farm, able to grow something of this and something of that, sunflowers, peanuts, cotton, a bit of maize, a bit of tobacco. Why did they choose that farm rather than any of the other vast expanses of bush? It was the hill on which the house was built, giving views for miles.

When they arrived in the colony the rainy season was soon to start: October, very hot indeed.

The family arrived in Salisbury, and were accommodated at a farm just outside in 'a guesthouse'. The place was Lilfordia, belonged to a man, Boss Lilford, who was later Ian Smith's friend, and loathed by the blacks. What could my parents have imagined as 'a guesthouse'? Some pretty cottage in Suffolk? There were ten or so large mud huts, grass-roofed, scattered on sandyish pink soil, fenced by poinsettias and hibiscus. Since these two knew nothing whatsoever about Africa, there had to be a government man to advise them.

Imagine the scene. In one of the mud huts, on a chair made of paraffin boxes with, if the maker aimed high, a seat of plaited rush – the kind of furniture she was making within a few weeks – there my mother sat. My father had already had interviews with the Land Bank, the Department of Agriculture.

My mother was wearing one of her Liberty dresses.

'When buying clothes remember the weather may be inclement. Cotton or linen will be best, with a woollen coat for the nights, which can get cold.'

The government man's father might have come up with the Pioneer Column thirty-five years before. He himself might have been an ex-serviceman, like my father. He might have come from South Africa: so many Rhodesians had escaped 'the troubles' on the Rand, always strikes, fighting, rioting.

It was his job to introduce Mrs Tayler to the problems of farming. He was unlikely to be or have been a farmer himself.

'Now, Mrs Tayler, what kind of a farm are you looking for?'
This young man had no idea of what he was up against.

First of all, what was my mother wanting? To live among 'nice people', people of our kind, 'our class of people' – all phrases used freely then, without embarrassment. In other words, middle-class people, who would share her tastes in music, and whose children would be provided with the books children must have. Did she use the words 'people of our sort' to this colonial? She was capable of it. If so, he must have been more than offended. 'You see, Mrs Tayler, this colony doesn't go in for that kind of thing,' he might have said, or implied. 'You'll just have to take your chances.'

Now this was my mother's chief and dearest demand for her life in Southern Rhodesia. If it could not be like Kenya, about which she knew nothing, well, then, 'our kind of people' were always, surely, everywhere?

Middle class, music loving, caring about literature and politics – which meant Tory. And art.

Did she actually say these things? Surely not. Art? She had brought with her an enormous book of the Impressionists, which was to give me so many hours of pleasure. She would surely have to doubt that this youth could have heard of the Impressionists.

'My husband would want to ride about the farm,' she must have said.

Was it this government man from Salisbury who actually settled them – remember the *kopje* on which the house would be built? They needed advice, so much, but I don't think they got it.

Horses did not do well on our side of the District, where the earth was mostly heavy, some of it the heavy red and black soils famous for their productivity. Horses in that District were on the other side, on sand veld. No one had horses near us, but there were two donkeys for a while, and my father rode one. For a while.

The requisition for 'the nice people' failed at once. The neighbours, all solidly working-class Scots, were not within my mother's definition of 'our kind' and found her snobbish, definitely not one of them.

There were half a dozen people in the District who came to the music evenings. They were nice people, but they were also war victims. Two had wooden legs, one a wooden arm; one was a war widow.

And there was the question of the actual land not being enough. And there wasn't water – no river. For years the farm managed with three inadequate wells.

There was no way my parents could have returned to England when they did understand the farm's unsuitability.

My father had his war pension; the thousand pounds that was his capital had been swallowed buying equipment for the farm.

What would they do in England? The slump that would soon begin would answer that. My mother was getting on towards fifty when my father was struck by diabetes.

Ten years on from the start on the farm, the emotional balances had changed in the family.

First, my brother. My mother was convinced that I would be a boy, and didn't even have a name for a girl. My brother, when he was born, was her heart's delight, and of course I knew it.

'He is my baby.' Fair enough, when he was little, but she called him Baby and went on, Baby Harry, Baby, Baby, until he, aged seven, said to her, 'You must not call me Baby.'

'But you are my baby,' she wailed humorously, being in the right, but my father stepped in.

'You must stop,' he commanded. 'It's not fair to him.'

My brother stuck it out. She insisted on Baby, so he would not hear her, would not respond, and there was my father, so seldom adamant in matters of the family, but angry and adamant now.

My mother had lost her baby. My father had not yet succumbed to illness, but here was her daughter, and now began the struggle with me.

So much has been written about mothers and daughters, and some of it by me. That nothing has ever much changed is illustrated by the old saying, 'She married to get away from her mother.' *Martha Quest* was, I think, the first no-holds-barred account of a mother-and-daughter battle. It was cruel, that book. Would I do it now? But what I was doing was part of the trying to get free. I would say *Martha Quest* was my first novel, being autobiographical and direct. My first novel, *The Grass is Singing* was the first of my *real* novels.

I saw this recently. A woman, an actress, had a daughter and then a boy. The girl had never seen her mother otherwise than as a housewife, and pregnant, or nursing, overweight – her mother, her possession, *her* mother. The actress, returning to work in a play where she was a glamorous lead, took the little girl to see her on the first night. The mother was proud of returning to what she felt was her real self, smart, attractive, well dressed. The little girl sat in the front row with her father, silent and tight-faced. At the end of the play, asked by a well-meaning friend, 'Didn't you feel proud to see your mother up there on the stage, looking so wonderful?', she burst out, a dam of emotion at last allowed its head, 'Her? Oh, she wasn't anything, she wasn't much, she isn't anything *really*.'

There you have the elemental rivalry, all out in the open, no concealment.

I hated my mother. I can remember that emotion from the start, which it is easy to date by the birth of my brother. Those bundling, rough, unkind, impatient hands: I was afraid of them and of her, but more of her unconscious strengths.

I was six when I ran away for the first time. Running away in the middle of the bush is not like some escape in a big city or a village. I ran in the middle of the night down the track to the bigger track to the station. There were animals in the bush, leopards in the *kopjes*, and snakes. I was crying and noisy with fury. I had no money. I knew that when – *if* – I got to the station, they would not allow me on to a train. I was afraid and went meekly back home and into bed without anyone knowing. I did it again. This was a cry for help, like cutting one's wrists or taking an overdose. My mother's way of dealing with it was to ring up neighbours and, with fond laughter, tell them of my exploits. 'She got as far as the Matthews turn-off. What a silly child.'

It would never have occurred to her to think that she might be at fault. And this brings me to a really vast subject, not, I think, much acknowledged. There has been a change, an enormous one, in medicine, drugs, but a greater one in popular consciousness of ordinary psychology. The words 'a cry for help' are part of ordinary knowledge in parent-child interaction. I am sure they had 'problem children' always, even problem parents, but not understood in the way of ordinary advice in newspapers, or how any run-of-the-mill parent is judged.

Running away, the furious criticism implied in it, was made bland by her laughing at it.

I told her, not much older, that she was not my mother, who was in fact the Persian gardener (I remember him as a kindly and, above all, just presence). I knew, of course, that the gardener, being male, could not be my mother, but necessity somehow overruled this disability. And that brings me to the wonderful way children both know and do not know the facts, can believe in a fairy tale with one part of their minds and know it is not true with the other. It is a great, nourishing, saving ability, and if a child doesn't achieve this capacity it may be in trouble.

I told my mother I hated her. Many children do, and no harm comes of it. My mother could not come to harm because she was, by now, only a mother. That was all Fate had allowed her to be.

The hating and not hating are again parts of mental double dealing: when I was sent away to board I was in miseries of homesickness. If I was not sick for my mother, then what? It was the farm, the dogs, my father, later my brother when he was there, and the weeks stretched themselves out as weeks did then, and I savoured every minute of the holidays, and yet I was in continual fights with my mother.

So all that went on – 'Only family life', as some people would say – while I dreamed of getting out, getting away, getting out from under.

And then I was thirteen and something very good happened, the best. I got measles, and with ten or so other girls was put into an empty house, without supervision, with medicines, meals brought in from the hospital and a nurse dropping in every day or so to look us over.

In those days quarantine for measles took six weeks. They put us on our honour not to go near any unauthorized person.

Towards the end of the time some girls fretted, but if you are covered with a rash and feeling low there is little inducement to be seen by anyone. A couple of girls put on bathing costumes, lay around on the lawns and practised a haughty indifference to the boys who sometimes leaned along the fences, jeering. But all around the garden were big notices: 'Quarantine for Measles, Keep Out'. That was such a good time. Perfect isolation, peace, no pressures. I understood how

I could be, how life might be. Letters came in. My mother wrote every day, saying she was arranging tutoring for this, lessons in that. Her letters made me wild with anger. Then she arrived at the perimeter fence, and gesticulated: she was leaving food parcels. We were stuffing ourselves with the good food they sent in, and did not need cake and sweets.

As usual, when I actually saw my mother, a lonely, unhappy, ill-looking woman, and her pleading eyes, I was wild with pity for her, and I wished, oh, wished, she would not come into town, send food, write letters. We were supposed to be doing homework; exercises of all kinds arrived regularly. I don't remember us doing any. We sat about, tried on each other's clothes – do not imagine the clever clothes there are now; none of us had much, a dress, a blouse, slacks. We talked, we did nothing, we dreamed. Of all the lucky things that have happened to me in my life, this dose of measles counts as one of the best. But it ended, and back in school I got pink-eye, an affliction causing infinite witty teasing, but it was no joke. I thought I was going blind. And then it was the holidays and I left school for ever, not knowing I had, or why, only that I had reached the end.

Back on the farm things could not have been worse: to balance the perfect bliss of the long freedom of quarantine. I said my eyes were damaged and I could not read, but I read as much as ever.

My father had just been diagnosed with diabetes and was very ill. In those early days of diabetes they did not know how to treat it. My mother was ill all the time. She had 'neuralgia', 'sick headaches', 'a heart'. Both had cupboards full of patent medicines. I succumbed with a variety of dubious ailments, and could have spent my life as they did, absorbed by my health, but there was another lucky thing. A charity sent the children of settlers for holidays, and I was rescued from the miseries of that house and was in a wonderful mountainous place, in the house of an old woman, Granny Fisher, eighty years old, who could walk any of her paying guests off their feet. Illness was forgotten.

When I had to return to the farm it was only a question of when I would leave it.

Now I watch the struggles of adolescents with such feeling: their efforts to be themselves are often pathetic, foolish and misguided; they often know as little of what they are doing as I did, but they have to try, struggle, get free.

I had to get free. My battles with my mother were titanic. What were they about? Everything, nothing, but she was going frantic as I escaped her.

You won't let me live through you, you won't let me be you, you are killing me.

And I: No, I won't. Let me go. No, I won't – do whatever it was she had planned for me.

During those few months she had decided I was to be a great pianist (as she could have been) but I had no talent; a great singer – but I had no voice; a great artist ...

I would go along with some flight of fancy, and then common sense struck home again and I would brutally point out: *But I have no talent.*

Was I telling her she had no talent? What was I saying? Only, 'No, I won't.'

She was demented at that time, poor woman. Her husband was ill. Her precious son, 'Baby', had run away from her long ago, and I was saying, No, no, no, no.

She was a very talented woman in many different ways. I have never met anyone as efficient as she was, such an organizer. All her talents, her energy were narrowed down to one graceless, angry girl who had only one idea, which was to leave her.

And so I did. I was what is now called an au pair for two years, but she never left me alone, wrote interminable letters to whomever I was working for, telling them how to treat me.

Only one good thing happened to me in that time: I had been reading, rereading, had been sunk in a slow dream of the books of my childhood, but I suddenly realized I had not read anything serious or grown-up except war books for years. So now I began ordering books from England for myself, embarked on the great and glorious discovery of literature, an adventure that has gone on through my life. But I owe to her, my mother, my introduction to books, reading – all that has been my life. No, she would not understand now the books I read, because they had played no part in her life. H. G. Wells, Bernard Shaw and Maeterlinck were where she stopped, with the memoirs of generals and of the battle fronts everywhere.

She would finger the books I had ordered from London and was suspicious. Everything I did seemed a snub and an affront to her, and so it was, whether I intended it or not.

Writers and poets have all claimed that the impact of the great Russian writers changed them. This was true of all Europe. I don't remember why I knew enough to order Tolstoy, Chekhov, Dostoyevsky, Turgenev and the rest, but I had the news from somewhere and I read and was amazed. No books have ever had such an effect on me as the great Russians. I think the perennial cry, 'The novel is dead,' is because none of us has written anything as good as *War and Peace*, *Anna Karenina* and Dostoyevsky. Quite simply, they represent the peak and glory of literature. There have been a thousand learned articles explaining the reasons for this, but for me the fact of it is enough.

I was ordering books mentioned in other books; I had no guide. And slowly through the thirties and then the war years, when parcels of books had to dodge the U-boats, I ordered books from England, and the arrivals of the parcels were the high points of my life. From the Russians, then, to the French, with Stendhal my great love, and Balzac, and Zola.

The American writers were almost as much of a thrill as the Russians. Theodore Dreiser – but it seems no one reads him these days, yet he has written some great novels – Steinbeck, Dos Passos, Hemingway, but him with less admiration, *The Great Gatsby*, but I think Scott Fitzgerald wrote only one great novel; Faulkner, but he came later, and then the English writers, but I had already read most of them by then. Hardy has ever been a favourite, George Meredith – also out of fashion – Daniel Defoe, George Eliot, the Brontë sisters, Jane Austen, and the mad, wonderful *Tristram Shandy*. What have

I left out? The poets, but I had been given them early. And far from last on my list was Proust, an improbable passion, and I read and reread *The Remembrance of Things Past*, knowing it was an antidote to what I actually lived in – Rhodesia at war, the last throbs of the British Empire – though no one would have believed that possible then.

Virginia Woolf and D. H. Lawrence, but not all of these were easily got. For instance, *Lady Chatterley's Lover* was an expurgated edition. Periodicals produced with great difficulty in paper-rationed England were *New Writing* and *New Writing and Daylight*.

I have, of course, left out a lot, but this list represents what people were reading then, if they read at all. And here it is, for what it is worth, but I feel it will already be seen as a survivor from a quaintly old-fashioned past.

My mother's letters to me were dreadful. Only a mad woman could have written them. That I was embarking on the career of a prostitute was only one of her accusations. Even then I knew she was ill, and I would tear up the letters as they arrived. It was probably the menopause. These days she would not have suffered as she did. I keep coming back to the same thing: now, the clever medicine we have would have seen her through.

That I was saving myself by escaping from her I did know, but had no idea of just how powerful is the need to take over a child's life and live it. And back we must go to her confrontations with her father.

John McVeagh was the ideal father. He gave his children

everything that an Edwardian father should. They were taken to see every public event, like the visit of the Emperor of the Germans to London, the parades, royal birthdays, tattoos, the Relief of Mafeking. My mother's memory was like an almanac of official occasions. She went to a good school. She had everything in the way of concerts and theatre, she played hockey and tennis, and was brilliant at the piano. But there was a point when this idolized girl stood up and said, 'No, I won't.' Why did she have to? John McVeagh, unusually for his time, wanted his clever daughter to go to university. It had to be the girl, and not the boy, who wasn't good enough. His ambitions therefore were focused on her, the one who passed examinations and was always at the top of the class. But she said, 'No,' to him and went off to be a nurse, which made him say, apparently without any consciousness of the absurdity of it: 'Never darken my doors again,' and 'I shall no longer consider you my daughter.'

Now, there is something inexplicable here. The Royal Free Hospital was training women doctors: why did she not decide to be a doctor? Her father would surely have been pleased – but I have answered the question. Precisely: her father would have been pleased. So, no, she would be a nurse and 'wipe the bottoms of the poor'.

But why? I cannot remember her saying anything that could elucidate. She didn't like her stepmother but she never said much about her, except that she was cold and a disciplinarian. How extraordinary, then, that Emily McVeagh stood up to her father and said, 'No.' But the real question surely has to be, Why did that fat papa of a man, that burgher, have to see his clever daughter as his continuation, his justification?

How strange that she never explained it, or perhaps did not see it as needing explanation.

There was this obedient little girl, obeying her father in everything, afraid of disappointing him, standing in front of him as rigid as a ruler, arms down by her sides, waiting for praise or blame (and she acted this scene for me so I could see her, and the stern, powerful father). And all that went on and went on, while she did better and better and won applause for everything, was told she could have a career as a concert pianist if she wanted, was clever Emily McVeagh, and then – finish – she said, 'No, no, no, NO.'

John McVeagh's first wife, Emily Flower, had died, and left him with three little children, one a disappointing boy, and his second wife was probably not an armful of fun. But there was his clever girl, who triumphed over everything. So, suppose she had gone to university, done very well, emerged with honours and applause. Studying what? Something he had chosen for her. Is that what he was dreaming of to make his own life end in achievement? But we shall never know. What influences did Emily McVeagh have that caused her to choose nursing of all things? 'But nurses are not of our class, Emily' – choosing nursing to fulfil herself.

And now her daughter was saying, 'No,' tearing up her letters, was running from her as fast as she could, a flight culminating in that ancient resort of girls beset by their mothers, 'Well, of course I got married to get away from my mother.'

A Women's Group, Informal, Casual

Now fast forward to the war years, and the problems of young women, fifteen or so of us. Then they were to be distinguished by their politics, all socialist or Communist, and that was how they saw themselves. On meeting anyone they would at once say, 'I am a member of the Party'; 'I joined when Hitler attacked the Soviet Union'; or 'I left the Party when Stalin attacked Finland'; or 'on the Hitler–Stalin Pact'; 'I am a Marxist Communist'; or 'I know Marxists cannot be Zionists, but I am a Marxist Zionist.'

What has to strike one is that they were all so well-read – compared with now, remarkably so. Nowadays, minds rotted by TV or the Internet, it is not rare to read a reviewer saying, apparently with pride, that he, she, cannot read *War and Peace* because it is long; or *Ulysses,* because it is difficult. Then it would not occur to readers to confess incapacity. When it was agreed that there was a prob-lem we shared, it was natural for us to approach it from literature. I cannot remember any other time when there were women-only meetings, but this was because men simply would not understand.

Each of us had a mother, and not merely on that level where a girl may roll her eyes and say, 'It's my mother, you know.' It was a serious business, and we began, saying that to judge by literature, plays, memoirs, there had recently been dominating bullying fathers, whose sons and daughters were afraid of them. Where had they gone? In their places were neurotic mothers, driving their daughters mad. One mother, apparently fixated on 1920s flappers, wore short skirts, dangling necklaces, a foot-long amber cigarette holder, and she was at her daughter's every morning by breakfast and there she stayed until night. The daughter was married and the way the mother dealt with the unfortunate reality was to ignore the husband, saying, 'You only married him to annoy me, anyway.' She was an extreme.

Some girls had come out to the colony, as the custom then was, to get a husband, but the war had blown the Rhodesians up north to fight Rommel and survive or not. The colony was now full of the RAF, the English, but to marry one of them meant, as they saw it, a bit of a defeat. Their mothers' letters from England pleaded with them to get a husband. Two mothers had followed their daughters out to Salisbury, both apparently believing that this move in itself meant the daughters should live with them and support them. My mother – but enough.

'Marry to get away from my mother?' What a joke. When she visited me, she would move the furniture, throw out any clothes that displeased her, nag the servants and give orders to the cook. 'And why didn't you ever say no to her?' demanded the therapist to whom I was driven, years later.

'It would have been like hitting a child,' was what I said, but if I said something like, 'Mother, you really must accept the fact some time that I am grown-up now,' she would reply, 'But you are so hopeless, you have no idea at all.' My husband laughed. I could not appeal to my father, who was too ill.

So, how did these pathetic demented women come about? Well, we knew. How intelligent were our discussions, illustrated by a hundred examples from novels, but I cannot remember if our ever-so-clever analyses changed anything. We knew what the trouble was. These were women who should have been working, should have worked, should have interests in their lives apart from us, their hag-ridden daughters.

And when not long ago in England there was a pronouncement that women should not work, should be at home, caring for their children, I wondered how many women, like me, wanted to cry out: 'Stop! You're mad. You don't know what you're doing. Do you really want to create another generation of women who cannot let their children go? Is that what you want?'

All our mothers, looked at for their potential, were capable women, one or two extraordinarily so, and they should have been lawyers, doctors, Members of Parliament, running businesses.

All, every one, bemoaned their lot like this: 'I should have been a singer ... an actress ... a great artist ... a dress designer ... a model ... but I got married. I was too young to know what I was doing. Children finish you – they put an end to anything you could have been.'

And now there are women, more and more, who decide not to have children, and what a great thing that is.

If you want to imagine a fate worse than death – yes, that's not going too far – take a woman, without maternal instincts, let's say in the nineteenth century, or in any past century when there was no birth control. She would have to get married, and then have children, because there was nothing else for her. A woman who should never have had children had a brood, and no escape, unless she was tough-minded enough to choose to be a spinster.

This was the kind of thing our women's group discussed. We were very far from modern feminists: our discussions did not do much to change our mothers, if they did help us to put up with them.

I look back at the mothers of my generation and shudder and think, Oh, my God, never, never let it happen again … and I look back at my mother and know that what she really was, the real Emily, died in the breakdown she had soon after she landed on the farm. For a long time I knew I had never known my father, as he really was, before the war, but it took me years to see that I had not known my mother, as she really was, either. The real Emily McVeagh was an educator, who told stories and brought me books. That is how I want to remember her.

At various times in that long decline away from everything she knew herself to be, my mother accepted that her fate was to be a mother and 'That was that!' Then her incomparable driving energy would focus again on me – my brother had escaped her – and make plans for my instruction. And don't imagine I'm not grateful. Of course I could – and did – enquire loudly that if she intended me to go to 'a good school' in England, then why did she make me learn farm matters?

My going to school in England was part of what I and my brother called 'getting-off-the-farm', not scornfully, although we knew it was moonshine, but with no comprehension of her, or my father, for we had not been trapped: no slimy tentacle had come up from the depths to grab our ankles and drag us down, down. 'Getting-off-the-farm' did not depend for them on selling a good crop of maize or tobacco, but on winning the Irish sweepstake, or finding gold.

Thus I would be told I must look after a sitting hen 'from start to finish', or be responsible for the orphan calf, or 'take total charge' of feeding the chickens for a week. 'You have to know how things really are,' my mother would insist, eyes flashing. 'On the warpath,' my father said. And so, I do, and I thank her for it.

My Black Calf

Our pretty cow is Daisy Moo.
I love our friendly cow.
She tries with all her heart
To give us milk and yellow cream
To eat with apple tart.

I think few in the world would recognize this friendly cow.

'A herd of cows' – and we see them up to their middles in sweet English grass and clover, contented.

The milking herd on our farm in Africa was six or seven lean, drought-racked creatures: you needed half a dozen to provide enough milk for the house; in England one would be more than enough.

But there aren't contented clover-eating cows now that we treat them so cruelly, lock them up and feed them what we will. They never saunter through rich grass, never breathe real fresh air, and their udders hold gallons of milk, an unnatural thing, which keeps them on the verge of collapsing from illness. These cows would envy the lot of our haggard, bony beasts: their existence would seem paradise to them.

A small boy tended the house cows, keeping an eye open for a leopard or dogs, and in the worst time when milk was so short, my mother asked him if he was giving milk to his family, though of course he did and would until the rains came and brought the grass.

Our cows were sharp-horned, wild-eyed survivors, and if I came on them when walking I kept my distance.

No tame house pets, no friendly cows, and their cream was just enough to keep the family in butter, nothing like the rich cream my parents would remember: 'Now, in England ...'

A heifer would be driven across to a neighbour who had a bull, which must not be imagined as the kind that gets ribbons at fairs, and returned sanctified for motherhood. A cow worn out with her hard life would be sent to the butcher after she had had perhaps two or three calves.

One day two calves, one black, the other black and white, were driven up to the house. The mother had died in calving and it was decided that we, the house on the hill, would raise them. To my father it was sentimental nonsense; my mother said it would be good for us, 'us' being my brother and me, but he did not play his part. The black calf, a male, was mine and I must look after it.

Little milk came up in the pails in that cold dry season, but some was splashed into a basin, and I introduced my fingers into the calf's mouth. The suction and pull on my fingers seemed then, and still does, like a cry from the very heart of hungry need – *Let me live. I must live.* If I were in a world stripped by war or famine, so that nothing was left, and I thought of that frantic sucking, I would have to believe that life must triumph. The calf sucked so hard my fingers were white, and my mother said, 'Good God, he'll have the blood out of them.' She was reproving the calf. *Give me, give me, give me* ...

Soon there was no milk left and the calf was butting at my legs desperate to bring down the milk from his dead mother.

We sent a man on a bicycle to the store and he brought back containers of powder, and these, being converted into milk, were offered to the calf, and soon he had outgrown my fingers and his whole muzzle was in the bowl. He drank and he drank and his backside and his sister's were streaked with diarrhoea, and my father said, 'You'll kill those calves.' But the calves adjusted and they drank their reconstituted milk and it was never enough, at least for my calf, named Demi. They were named after the twins in Louisa M. Alcott's stories, Demi and Daisy.

How Daisy got on I do not remember, so absorbed was I with this imp of a little calf, who stood under a bush with her, waiting for my appearance, which meant milk.

He was such a handsome little calf, glossy, supple, black and shiny, and his hindquarters and tail wriggled and frisked with delight at the milk and he was so pretty, such a delight ...

He was as beautiful as the black silk gloves that ... Yes, it might seem absurd, this raw little farm girl, talking about black silk gloves, but they existed. In the house, under the thatch, pushed against the mud walls, was a 'Wanted on Voyage' cabin trunk and in it were evening dresses and shawls, but on a tray at the top were fans, scarves, little sequined bags and gloves, some of white kid, and there were the black silk ones, with minute jet buttons to the elbow. No occasion, excursion, party I had ever experienced would have proved a setting for those gloves, which I marvelled over and worshipped as evidence that the world was not contained in our bush landscape in the middle of Africa, that other perspectives existed. Those gloves, lying in my rough little hands, limp, shining, as fragile as the shed skin of a snake ... they were, well, of the same order as the shiny black elegance of the little calf. What did they have in common? It was that they were a gift, unexpected, like the heavy opulence of the lilies that bloom for one day after the rains fall, carpeting the veld with flowers that look as if they come from a rainforest, not drought-bitten Africa.

The drought went on, the milk was always less in the pails, and inside that elegant black calf raged an unappeasable hunger. If he had been out on the veld with his mother he would not yet have tried grass, he was too young, but milk did not satisfy him.

And so my mother tried supplementary feeding, using the all-purpose, always-useful mealie-meal, ground maize, mixing it with a little milk. Both calves liked this food. Both were growing fast, and by the time the rains came and green poked through the old dried clumps, they were being fed with what was really diluted porridge. By now a panful was being cooked for them, and mixed with milk and water.

It has to be said these calves were a nuisance, charming as they were. They were like dogs, intruding everywhere like dogs, or lying with them under the shade bushes. Their droppings had to be cleaned up and put on the garden. You fell over calves in doorways, on paths. The dogs thought they were honorary canines and one might see a dog lick a calf's ear, or a porridge-crusted muzzle, or use the close-cropping snap-snapping of their teeth to kill fleas or ticks, and the calves stood still, nervous, jumping and jiving a little, but they did not run away. The dogs came freely in and out of the house, pushing open the swing doors, but the calves could not do that, though they tried.

They were growing fast. I tried to ride Demi. I made halters and bridles of strips of blankets, doubled and redoubled, but he snapped them at my first attempt, which left me lying bruised on the ground. He did not seem to hold it against me, though.

Meanwhile my father said we did not know what we were doing, and when these two were sent back down to the herd, the others would not accept them. We were setting up a sad life for these pets of ours, who seemed to do as they liked.

We had evolved dog biscuits, out of maize meal. We had never heard of polenta, but it was polenta we made. Long afterwards I read a description of how in an Italian kitchen the making of polenta was an occasion for the family to gather around. In our smoky kitchen, the black pot stood on the wood stove, bubbling, sending out the slightly acid smell of boiling water, and the maize meal, glittering gold, was trickled into the water and stirred until ... This was the unrefined maize meal, full of flavour, not the tasteless refined stuff that is popular now.

The baking tins were lined with dripping, which no longer exists. When beef was roasted on Sundays, it gave off a wonderful rich fat, which was set in bowls over an inch or two of dark jelly, to be eaten on toast. Or put into the baking tins for the dog biscuits. The maize porridge was smoothed down into the fat, marked in squares with a knife, sprinkled with coarse salt and baked. It was delicious. We children snatched what we could, so did the servants, the dogs waited in the kitchen for the stuff to cool, and the calves came to get their share. More and more had to be made of these dog biscuits, so crisp and salty and good, and the calves ate every scrap they were given.

You would see a calf and a dog trying to nose each other out of the way of a square of the stuff and my calf, who was pretty big by this time, might push a dog over.

'They will have to go back to the herd,' said my father, but we delayed, or I did. I was fond of my unruly, bossy great calf.

I used to sleep with my door open, held by a stone. This was despite the dogs that might jump in, and more than once a snake. I could not bear to close that door. My bed looked across the bush to the mountains of the Dyke, coloured blue and rose and mauve, where the sun came up.

One night I woke and there in my room stood my calf, and he seemed undecided what to do. There was an empty bed between him and me, and he was about to shoulder his way into my parents' room. I had to push him from my room, the great beast. My father spoke. 'Enough,' said he. 'We can't have herds of cattle roaming through the house.'

'But he's only ...' began my mother, about to say that he was only a calf.

But he wasn't.

Down they went, the young black ox – he was nearly that – and his pretty black and white sister. The herd did not seem to mind. But the pair did badly. My calf did not become a young bull: his testicles were wrong, and he would not be inspanned or yoked. He seemed to remember a high place where the winds blew, not this bush where the heat bit like a scorpion. There the dogs didn't chase you, as they did here, but licked your ears and bit off the ticks. There were caresses, and many little treats. He wasn't going to be an ordinary old trek ox, not him. Then his sister calved, perhaps too young, and her calves both died.

So, not a success, then.

When I wandered about on the farm, I kept a lookout for my calf, and one day there was a thunder of hoofs and towards me came a big black ox with scything horns and the intention, surely, to renew old friendship. I ran to the nearest ant heap, luckily a tall one, and went up it. The ox stood looking up, but I had vanished.

Those horns ... Once I had rubbed the bristling little lumps while the calf lowered his head for me. His budding horns were uncomfortable. Did he remember, while he tossed those murderous horns about and bellowed, then wandered off again?

My poor Demi was a useless creature. When I was at school, they made a feast of him for the labourers, and they did not tell me. I was careful not to ask. For years, wandering out by myself, I would imagine I heard the thunder of hoofs and see that great, clumsy, affectionate beast charging up to me.

But at the back of my mind was a summons, not to 'a good school in England' but to a life so far from anything in Banket, Southern Rhodesia, that it had all the glamour of Never Never Land. It was summed up by the brown fibre 'Wanted on Voyage' trunk that sat behind a curtain in my parents' bedroom.

In there were clothes as good as anything in the rare fashion magazine that might be blown into the house. To touch them, play with them, yearn over them was what I begged for. And my mother said, 'No, no. What for? What good would it do you?' and 'You aren't going to learn anything useful, pawing over my old frocks.'

But then, one day, just like that, she said yes; some new disappointment must have overtaken her, telling her that, no, she would never wear those frocks, those feathery boas, the brocade shoes, the satin evening cloaks, whose hems were weighed with deep strips of diamante or embroidery.

The middle part of the trunk held the frocks, and as we opened it, moths flew up.

'I should have put in more mothballs,' remarked my mother, as dry as you like, almost indifferent, just as if she was not about to see her precious dreams for the frocks disappear into moth holes. She sat there, my mother, while my avid grubby clumsy hands took off layers of crisp white paper – well, not so crisp now. I laid on the floor a sage green lace dress, with long sleeves and, in the front, covering a deep V, a wisp of the palest pink chiffon, or some scrap of flesh-coloured stuff. 'A dinner dress,' murmured my mother. 'I never actually wore it. It was too formal for the voyage.' A dinner dress! People wore clothes especially made to eat their dinner in? 'It's for a dinner party, you see,' she remarked, in that offhand voice, dry from keeping the tears at bay.

There it lay, on the floor, the tissue paper in rolls and puffs around it.

It was mid-calf, 1924. Since then skirts had climbed to the knee and were low again, on the dresses that were winsome and girlish and feminine. I took out a slithery mass, which, laid on top of the sage dinner dress, then lifted up to see, consisted of two sheets of midnight blue sequins, back and front, on a backing of dark blue chiffon.

'I wore that,' murmured my mother, 'on the last night of the voyage at the captain's table. People noticed it.'

I held it up. It was heavy. 'Just look at those gorgeous sequins.' Tiny holes appeared in the chiffon. The sequins dragged in places because the moth had got at the material they were stitched on.

That was a dress to admire, not to love.

The next was a dark blue confection, with a plain round-necked top, falling from the hips in layers of tulle, or chiffon, or something like that. The moths had had a real go at those skirts.

'That's a ball dress,' she remarked, 'but since I bought it, there hasn't been a ball.'

Then came a black lace dress, the skirt again falling from the hips, over an emerald green lip. There were lace sleeves to just above the elbow.

The idea would be, said my mother, instructing me, to wear a bracelet under the lace on one arm.

'I see,' I said.

And then *the frock*, the beauty of them all, held up by me so that she could see it. It had the palest grey top, of chiffon, and on the chiffon were traceries of crystal beads. The lowest part, from the hips, was of slightly darker grey, like water rather than mist, and the crystalline tracery on that was a little heavier. The top had wide straps, made of the material with crystals on it folded over. There was a wisp of a little jacket, designed to show the patterns of beads.

'Oh, oh,' I moaned, 'just look, oh, just look.'

And she did just look, and saw … 'I've never worn it,' she said. 'When I saw it hanging there I knew it was my dress. I had to have it, I paid much too much …' and she put out her hand, a fine, elegant hand, worn with farm work, and stroked it.

It was full of moth holes.

There was another dress, of fine green linen. Like the others it flared from the hips to a hemline marked by a deep band of white embroidery. The neckline and the sleeves had the embroidery too.

But when and where would one wear it?

'Imagine,' said my mother, dry as the dust that hung in the air, 'what people would say if I put that on in Banket.'

'But what is it for?'

'That's a garden-party dress.'

A garden party!

'You know the park in Salisbury? Well, imagine it with English trees, and English shrubs and flowers. There would be music, you see, and a big marquee with tea and refreshments.'

And now she was crying, and wiping her eyes.

A dress in georgette – something delicate.

'Look, autumn colours,' said my mother, 'just like a beech wood in autumn.'

The skirt was to mid-calf, in 'handkerchief' points, each one defined by a brown bead.

'I suppose I could wear that here – if there was a party. No, not really.'

'I'm being very silly,' she announced, and swept herself up to her feet. 'You'd better have these,' she said. 'You can use them for dressing up. Or cut them up, if you feel like … I don't care …' and she ran out of the room to find a place to cry, I suppose.

A dress in silver lamé: the material was silver threads and black woven together. It was going black in patches. It smelled deathly. It had black jet beads around the neck and armholes. They were falling off. They lay scattered about over the other dresses, the floor, like tiny black ants.

And so those lovely frocks did get cut up, and when I was older with a few more inches grown, I tried to put what was left of them on.

But they were not what I wanted to wear, for nineteen-twenties fashions were being mocked, jeered at, ridiculous. It was not till the sixties and the mini-skirt that anyone had a good word to say for those low-waisted frocks.

When I wore one wrapped around my twelve-year-old, thirteen-year-old person, or saw the dog wearing the grey chiffon with crystal beads, which I and my brother put on him, as a joke, my mother looked hard and saw me, dressed in the uniform of an English girls' school, because 'getting-off-the-farm' had more potency with every year that passed and was further away.

If my mother dreamed sometimes aloud of London, herself as a girl or young woman, going with friends to a play, to the Trocadero, concerts, picnics in the parks, my father dreamed too, but while he would go along with her flights – 'Oh, imagine if we were there now, in Piccadilly' or 'Do you remember the chestnut seller?' – he was dreaming of very different landscapes.

Often I, my brother or both were sent down to the lands with a bottle of cold tea to find my father. We might pass the labourers watched by the boss-boy, and find my father, by himself, watching … It might be a chameleon's slow swaying progress along a branch, or weaver birds making their nests over water, in the wet season, or, in a wooded corner that was usually full of spiders, a web that stretched from tree to tree, the spider, a nasty black and yellow job, on guard in a corner.

My father was fascinated by spiders, but I stayed behind his shoulders where the spider could not leap out at me. The sheet of web would quiver as an insect landed on it, and the spider ran on its strong black legs to grasp it. In a minute the moth or beetle would be folded in sticky web and positioned where later the spider would come. 'Imagine,' my father might say, 'how that moth must be feeling. It can't move. I wonder if it can see the spider there. It's just as well we are all so shut inside ourselves. Imagine if we could feel what that poor moth is feeling. It would be awful.' I liked going down – bicycling or walking – to find my father, who might even say, 'I don't want to stop watching this spider,' or a bird feeding a nestling. 'I'll come up for lunch a bit later.' But then he got diabetes and he had to come up, to inject himself with insulin and test his urine, standing near the little spirit lamp, holding the test-tube over the flame.

'I sometimes think he doesn't really want to get off the farm,' my mother would say, hearing that, no, my father wouldn't come to lunch now – 'There's a spider, you see.'

Keeping my father in insulin was a precarious business. It was made somewhere in South Africa. The makers put a parcel of it on the train north, and at Salisbury somebody went to intercept it, and later put it on the train to Banket. It reached the post office, and the man telephoned to say the precious stuff was waiting. Another man on a bicycle, or we, the family, went in to get the insulin. No refrigerator. There was a contraption used by many farmers before they could afford one. A great tall box, a safe, with sides of doubled chicken wire, stood in tins of disinfectant to keep out the ants, in a shady place. Between the wire sides was a layer of charcoal. All round the top of the safe were little runnels of tin, with holes. These were kept full of water, which leaked down through the charcoal. Except on the very hottest days, yes, it kept cool, but there was always worry about the insulin.

When my parents did at last move into Salisbury the whole business of diabetes eased because there was a refrigerator.

If it was no longer so easy for my father to spend hours down on the lands, watching, contemplating, more and more did he like to sit out in front of the house, watching. He would watch the veld fires burn their slow way on the hills that were four or so miles away. Or, putting his head back, watch the heavens. I was allowed to stay up, and then my brother too, because 'It will be good for you.' We lay back in our deck-chairs, like my father, counting the shooting stars. There were many. And the stars were bright and near. 'Look, there's the Southern Cross'; 'Look, there's Orion ... the Plough, the Pleiades ...' My mother kept saying, 'It's time for bed,' but my father would say, 'Let them be.' He was dazed with starlight, wonder, or if the moon was around, then the moonlight was like a spell, keeping us in our chairs.

'You'd never see anything like this in Piccadilly, old girl,' my father reminded my mother. 'Sometimes I think it's all worth it, these nights. Sometimes when I wake in the morning I think of the night coming, and sitting here ...'

'Worth it!' my mother would say, in a low voice, because what was he saying? That the long misery on the farm was justified by the moon, the stars ... Yes, he was saying it and probably thought it, too.

My brother and I cycled everywhere on the native paths through the bush, sometimes miles from home. Our favourite places were what were then called the Ayrshire Hills, where we

knew there were leopards. But in all the years of haunting those hills we only once saw a leopard, and that was its tail disappearing into a cave. But we did find Bushmen paintings, then of no interest to anyone, hardly noticed. There is a whole industry now, full of interpretations of those lively little figures on the underside of rocks, at eye level, or our eyes lifted because of a rock rabbit, or snake, or – we hoped one day – that elusive leopard, feet above where anyone could reach today, and there more wonderful pictures, of men and of animals, but it was the animals you had to admire. 'Just look at that – it's an eland, an ostrich.'

'An ostrich *here?* There must have been ostriches. You couldn't just *imagine* an ostrich, could you?'

The parents listened differently to our tales of the Bushmen paintings. My mother tended to feel that anything of interest here, on the farm, lessened the possibilities of getting off it, but my father was fascinated. 'All those hundreds of years – thousands, I shouldn't wonder, the Bushmen were here, it was the Bushmen who lived here …' And we imagined the little hunters running through the bush, in twos, threes, or in bands.

'They were here long before the Bantu.' That was how the blacks were then described. 'Waves of Bantu came down from the north, killing and plundering and …'

The word '*bantu*' means people, that's all.

'I wish I could see these paintings …' So it must have been before my father got diabetes and became so very ill. And my brother and I were ten, eleven, thirteen – that kind of age.

'I must see for myself ...' and while my mother expostulated, my father took his stick, and got into the car. We cycled ahead, so he could follow. The old car, the Overland, ground along on the rutty tracks, and then could go no further. My father got out, keeping his eyes on us, cycling just ahead. Then the bicycles could not go on as the ground lifted into rocky slopes, and we put them under a pile of brush and walked. A bicycle cost five pounds – a year of wages. To find an apparently abandoned one would have been better than a pot of gold to a labourer.

It is not hard for energetic children to clamber up through stones, rocks, fallen trees, but for my father it was hard. But on he went, slipping on swathes of yellow grass, stumbling over rocks. And on we went ahead, our eyes on a certain little rocky *kopje,* always looking back to see if this one-legged man could follow. We knew that wild pig liked this area, warthog, let alone snakes. But on my father went and towards the end of that precarious, for him, ascent, he was pulling himself up, grasping bushes, stumps, anything he could grab and hold on to. And there was the final granite slope up which he lay, inching himself along, and then the flattish earth under the great overhang of rock. Here the paintings were so far up that one had to imagine the little people propping tree trunks or even big piles of stones so they could reach their painting place. My father pulled himself the last few feet and said, 'Just look at that.' The animals of that far-off time were right before us, all kinds of buck – and was that a crocodile? A spotty flank – yes, a leopard, and yes, the ostrich, yes, it *was* an ostrich, people could mock as they liked.

There sat my father, staring. And then, having looked till he was tired, he turned himself around and looked back, over the bush, and there a long way off was the shambling house we lived in.

'I sometimes do think it's all worth it,' said my father, defiantly, as if he imagined my mother overhearing.

It is such magnificent country. I saw it again, not so long ago, and in my mind were the tribes of Bushmen, and then the Bantu, differently named now but certainly killing and plundering, since that is what humans do.

It was not, as a child, that I didn't know what a wonderful landscape I lived in – I knew it well enough – but going back after so long, it hit home hard. This was where I and my brother rode and ran and shot game for the pot. It was not our playground – you can't describe that serious bush-wise pair as children who played.

'My God,' said my father, staring, staring, at bush and *kopjes* and trees and hills and rivers …

And slowly we went back, down to where the bicycles lay concealed, to the old car and home.

My father described the Bushmen paintings to my mother. His mind was full of time, of history.

'Don't you see, old girl? It's like England. You know, we had Picts and Scots and Angles and Saxons and Vikings and the French … and each invasion raped and plundered and the priests killed the priests of the former invasion and there was a new set of kings and courtiers. Don't you see? It's just the same. The Bushmen lived here for thousands of years, some say, and then this lot came and then we came, the whites, and who after us? The Arabs, I shouldn't wonder, but someone will … And each wave destroys what was here before.'

Sister McVeagh

My mother's view of history was narrowed down to her daily task, which, though it was never called a clinic, or given any sort of descriptive name, was in fact a clinic, and she was its nurse.

Every morning, sitting all round the kitchen and sometimes well down into the bush, the labourers, men, women and children, waited for my mother. These people all, every night, slept in smoky huts where a log burned. They had their heads wrapped in blankets or cloth, and in the morning this waiting crowd could have been like a crowd of theatre extras told to say 'rhubarb'. The sound that came from them was 'Chefua, chefua', which means 'fire', and they pointed to their chests and their throats, telling my mother that they felt they were burning.

'Respiratory diseases,' my mother would say, sounding angry because she was impatient. 'Do they have to wrap up their heads, do they have to …' Yes, it is cold on the highveld (Kipling's word) in the winter, and cold when it rains. The burning smoky log is for heat. A burning log there has to be.

And that meant that among the people waiting for my mother every morning were babies who had toddled into the fire and were badly burned. If you looked at a crowd of labourers, their hoes rising and falling, there were always two or three with twisted or damaged legs and feet: they had been babies who had toddled into a fire.

'What am I to do?' demanded my mother of Fate, the Almighty, somebody. She provided aspirin and cough medicine and bound up the burned babies. Or she sent a note to the hospital in what was then Sinoia, Chinoia, and a whole family would go walking to the hospital with the burned baby on some woman's back.

'We can't afford it,' my mother would say. 'Do you realize? On what we spend on medicines for them, we could take a holiday, we could ...'

Other farmers' wives might dish out some aspirin or Epsom salts, but there was nothing like my mother's morning assembly anywhere near. People would come a mile, three, four, to sit on the earth and murmur, '*Chefua, chefua.*' Then the precious copper basin my parents had brought from Persia lost its status as a bedroom ornament and, setting it on the stool, my mother poured some aromatic or other into hot water and made the worst of the *chefua* sufferers, a towel over their head, sit and breathe in fire-killing fumes.

This was a popular attraction, but even more so was the stethoscope. They waited in lines to have the instrument hung around their necks and marvel at the sound of their own hearts.

My mother had the blackboard, on which she taught us arithmetic and spelling, brought out on its easel, and she drew a heart in red chalk. Standing in front of a crowd of Nyasas who knew no English, she instructed the cook to interpret. She explained the heart, its mechanisms, and used her two fists to demonstrate the pumping.

'Ah!' said the people. 'Ach!' Many exclamations.

My father watched, with the dogs sitting on their backsides, interested, and probably cats, and he said, 'Well now, old thing, and what do you think they have understood from all that?'

'But they have to know,' said Sister McVeagh, fierce, impatient. 'They have to know these things some time, don't they?'

'But when they catch a buck or a rabbit and they cut it up, they must see the heart then?' said my father.

'And what about the lungs? Their lungs must be black with woodsmoke.' To the cook, 'Tell them they simply must not breathe so much smoke,' said my mother.

My father said to the cook, 'What do you say the heart is for?'

This man spoke and understood a good bit of English. He did not read or write, though. 'The heart is for making the blood move,' said he. 'No heart, no good – dead,' he said, and added the word for 'death', and 'dead', in a variety of tones and languages. Everybody in the crowd laughed and clapped.

'There you are,' said my father.

But stethoscopes are not immortal and the one my mother

had brought from England gave up the ghost. She said she would order another, but then her clinic had to do without a stethoscope. Cough mixtures and Epsom salts and aspirin, ointments for the burned babies and splints for broken bones. And, kept handy because there were so many snakes, the snakebite outfit, which saved more than one life.

How was it my brother and I were not bitten? Now I marvel. But we were used to seeing a snake slither off into the grass, like the leopards' tails in the hills. I did once nearly pick up a puff adder, which specializes in looking slow and sleepy, but that was as near as I got to death by snakebite.

My father's mind slid so easily back into historical events, Bushmen, Bantu and who would succeed us whites, but I wonder what he would have said had he foreseen what was to come.

Fast forward, then! Forget the little brown hunters with their lethal bows and arrows, painting their lives and their animals on to every suitable rockface. Soon the family would leave the farm. It would be impossible to keep my father alive there: for one thing there were more comas and crises and rushed visits into town – if you can use the word 'rushed' for a deadly five-hour trip sliding from rut to rut over the difficult roads.

So they did 'get-off-the-farm' at last, did they? What a come-down, what an anticlimax! They went into a horrid little bungalow in a suburb, everything they both hated, and our farm was bought, its true status revealed by its being an annexe to a big farm. Our house did not last long. For years I had been used to seeing how, if there was a bush fire as close as a couple of miles, our house's thatch would be soaked in water ... but there was no water on our hill. Water came up by Scotch cart, two barrels on a wooden frame drawn by two oxen who strained up certain parts of the road. This bounty of water sat under a roof of thatch, for coolness, but when the fires were near, the oxen might be straining up and down that steep road half a dozen times in an afternoon. Against the thatch were laid ladders and tree-trunks and men ran up and down pouring water on to it. Then, if a spark did land, it must go out. But once the family left and the house was empty, the next fire sent a wave of flames from the bush – and up went that house, which now, it has to be admitted, was pure fantasy. Not that I saw that for years. Small children live in a reality that excludes the mad fantasies of adults.

I was adolescent before I actually saw that house, understood it ... A little girl does not see more than she can understand.

My mother had brought from Persia a cloth that, spread on a small table, was soon laden with books and ornaments, but the edges were visible. It was a khaki cotton, but the border was of small coloured pictures, appliquéd figures in subtle but strong colours. I would sit and marvel, the pictures at eye level. A donkey, and behind it a boy with a stick ... a man in a long dress wearing a tall, ugly black hat ... a tree with tiny red fruits ... a rosebush ... a woman with her head in a black shawl thing ... a snake – no doubt about it – with a red flickering tongue ... a large black bird, but then, as I edged my way

round the almost floor-length cloth, the donkey was repeated, black this time, and the bird, white instead of black.

I was learning to sew, with a kit that had come over the sea from England. Squares of material, gauze, hessian, something like floor matting, but for a doll's house, cotton, trouser material – khaki. I had a box full of needles, some of wood, almost the size of a finger, some metal, but blunted. And there were my attempts, stitches an inch long, on material that had puckered, despite my efforts. That was what I could achieve. 'Never mind, you'll do better.' But look at the pictures on this cloth's edge. Minute stitches, fairy stitches. On the black bird, the stitches were black, on the white donkey, they were tiny strokes of white; each picture had half a dozen different colours of thread, and what thread, as thin as a hair. That cloth's edge was a marvel. I sat there wondering and admiring, not believing that I – or any ordinary human – could ever do the same. Oh, just look, that tree, green as a tree is, had little blobs of red, and its companion tree on the other edge was green, but with yellow blobs, and the stitches were red and yellow and the stick the boy was going to hit the donkey with was not a thin streak of appliquéd cloth but was of black satin stitch. 'You see that there – that's satin stitch, it's used for filling in, yes, look over here ...' And another cloth showed large hanging fruits, yellow and orange and red, each filled in with the delightful tiny stitches. 'Satin stitch – you see?'

There was a large box, but perhaps it wasn't so very large, of brass, with figures on it of a dull metal, and here were scenes not unlike those on the cloth with its enticing edges. At least, here was a little donkey, here was a bird and, yes, a tree.

That is what a small girl sees, feels.

By the time I understood that house, the curtains were faded and fraying, and the coloured edges of the cloth had lost their brilliance. But what an extraordinary house my mother had created, back there in 1924, from trunks crammed full of plenty from Liberty's and Harrods. The floor was of shiny black linoleum, but as the tree roots rotted under it, hollows and bumps displayed the Persian carpets in ways their weavers had never intended. Those rugs had worn down to their elemental threads. But imagine that shiny black floor with the new wonderful Persian rugs ... The sitting-room walls my mother did not whitewash, because the greyish-brown of the mud set off the lively colour of the Liberty patterns. The cupboards and tables, all of black-painted boxes, were striking, combined with those patterns that my mother had seen long ago on Liberty's shelves. There were cushions, hangings and cloths from Persia, and some of their patterns are alive in my mind now. In the bedroom on the washstand was the wonder of a basin and jug in copper, which gleamed – this time against whitewash – but which had to be scrubbed and polished once a week because it went dull so fast, particularly in the rainy season.

In my room the curtains were of strong orange so that when the sun rose they flamed and burned …

This house, what a feat of the imagination it was … and what guests did my mother imagine she would entertain in it? They said, the parents, that it had been built to last four years – but how could that be? In four years they would have made all that money promised by the Southern Rhodesian stall at the Empire Exhibition and they would be able to get-off-the-farm and go back to England? No, no, none of it made sense, not to a scornful, accusing adolescent, who could acknowledge the charm, the impossible heartbreaking charm, of that old mud-and-thatch house, but since she was of the age for consistency, reason, sense, consequences, she simply could not accept that house as a reasonable thing.

Well, it wasn't.

And soon the flames swept in … and what did the many tiny inhabitants of the house do then? For in that thatch lived varieties of beetle and spider, the hornets made their nests in the walls, mice scurried in the rafters, the borers shed their white dust down on to the floor … I could imagine a tiny screaming and protesting, but that did no good, the house burned, and the next big wind would blow away the ashes. Who would ever know that here had stood this house of dreams, none of which included an ignominious 'getting-off-the-farm' into the suburb of a war-swollen town?

Insects

Sometimes the lower part of the crown of the hill was crowded with butterflies: the mysterious synchronicities of nature had meshed – the rains, the time of year, and that essential thing, plentiful cowpats on the track, since the water-cart had been up and down that morning, the oxen leaving their crusty sweet-smelling portions of – paradise. Sages of all denominations have used this vision thus: 'So, Master, to what can you compare this life of ours?'

'Our lives are as if a butterfly flutters in from the dark into a lighted place, sees beneath her a favourite food, flutters down and feasts on the ordure until she is replete – and then off she flies again into the dark.'

Probably the most exquisite sight I have ever seen is hundreds of butterflies, different ones, all sizes, fluttering their pretty wings and spread about over cowpats on the track.

Oh, what beauties, what a gorgeous sight, and the family stood as near as we could, marvelling. Then, one by one, off the butterflies drifted, back to their more ordinary delight: nectar.

If I choose to remember this vision, which I may do on a dark December afternoon in London, and not forgetting the benef-icence of the cowpats, I have to think too – honesty compels – of the other insects. Life is not, after all, exquisite butterflies with the afternoon sunlight on their wings.

Our house was in the middle of the bush, which was not twenty yards away in some places, and full of every imaginable insect. Some of them were a horror to me. One invasion was the worst. There is an insect, large, dark brown, with a bulbous body, and antennae, which came with the rains and was everywhere. My mother chided, the servants laughed at me, but I was sobbing, hidden in a corner. That was myself as a small girl, but I grew and the beetles, if that was what they were, went on appearing. I would be safe in my bed and then there they were on the mosquito net, a dozen of them, clinging with their little legs to the mesh, lopsided from the weight of their great bodies. I cowered under the bedclothes and screamed for help. My father, probably already in bed, laboriously arose.

'Your hysterical daughter is at it again,' he remarks, furious, but contained. He comes hopping on his clumsy crutch over the uneven floors and sees me crouching under the net, with the brown ugly things above me all over the net. He stands on one leg, holding on to the washstand with one hand, and brushes them off, using his crutch. They are scattered over the floor.

'No, no,' I cry. 'They'll climb up again, they'll get back on the net.' With what difficulty does my father reach for a towel, always holding on to the washstand, bend to scoop up the insects, which in my memory are emitting squeaks and complaints, then get to the door and shake them out into the night? 'Shut the door, shut the door,' I beg, though usually I did not allow that door to be shut.

He shuts it.

'What are you so frightened of?' he coldly enquires, turning with such an effort to manoeuvre himself and his crutch back to his room.

'Beetles,' he tells my mother, who has not budged from her bed: she thinks I should not be indulged in my irrational behaviour.

Well, what was I so afraid of to the point that I cowered, weeping, clinging to pillows?

There were other invasions, some I can hardly bear to remember.

In London Zoo they have classes for people with phobias. You become inured to furry, squeaking, hissing, biting things walking up your arms. Oh, no, no, don't even think of it.

If I have moments of sentimentalizing the bush, I make myself remember how, when walking quietly through the trees, I might find myself in the middle of a spider's web that clung like the poisonous one in an old myth or fairy story. The spider was vibrating with fury not an arm's length away.

An ugly bungalow was built further back from the brow of the hill, and then someone – who? – shortened the hill by about ten feet, or more. The old house had perched on the crown, and the ground had slid down all around it. The earth from this truncation was shovelled down the sides of the hill, where once the oxen had laboured, straining up steep sides.

And occupants came and went and left their mark: a line of neglected roses by a fence, some peach trees, which did not do well, any more than the pomegranates my mother had planted.

And then there was the Liberation War. All the farmhouses became fortresses, surrounded by tall security fences, locked and barred at night, but not so high it was impossible for terrorists or freedom-fighters to lob over a grenade, or even clamber over themselves. Inside the houses, I saw the rifles and shotguns laid on the windowsills, and buckets of water set out to deal with incendiary attacks. The white farmers in those beleaguered farmhouses had a long, frightening war, and then there was a black government, and so many misplaced hopes, and then the ugly little tyrant Mugabe. The security fences and siege weapons did not defend the inhabitants from these attackers.

And so my father, dreaming forwards instead of backwards, would have had to see all this District, once a byword for its efficiency, its wonderful crops of maize and tobacco, slowly begin to go back to the bush. For Mugabe's cronies, grabbing the white farms, were not thinking of feeding the population, providing for them. They left the farms unused. In order to keep farms healthy and productive you need fertilizers, machinery, and all kinds of experts. If it is a dairy farm, you need veterinary surgeons. Without these, there is nothing; neglect, and the lands going back to the bush.

The Old *Mawonga* Tree

Visiting the farm in the early eighties, I was standing perhaps fifty yards away from where the house was. In front of me swayed a drunk black man, tall, very thin, poorly dressed, reeking of stale beer. With me was Antony Chennells, then from the Zimbabwe University. He was the best of companions for such trips, apart from the fact that he knew as much about old Southern Rhodesian history, laws, literature, people, black and white, as anybody could. His grandfather was Charles Coghlan, the first prime minister of Southern Rhodesia. It was hard for me to come back to the farm, to the *kopje* where the house was – to my memories. We were there, standing before this angry man, without permission from the owners of the farm, because we knew we had only to ask to get permission, and because being there was something of an impulse.

'Why are you here?' says the drunk man, belligerent and accusing.

'Once I lived here. I was a child here,' I said, bright and breezy, as if this was not bound to be a pretty awful occasion.

He was too drunk to sneer properly, but he made the attempt.

I said, 'Our old house used to be there,' and I pointed to where bushes and even young trees were springing up.

I said, 'The people who came after us cut the top of this hill off. A good fifteen or twenty feet, it looks like.'

'No one has cut off the hill,' says the drunk.

He is, in fact, a mechanic, working for this annexe and the big farm it is now part of.

'I assure you,' I say, 'this hill is much lower than it was. They threw the earth down the sides of the hill. That is why the track up here isn't steep. It used to be so steep you had to change down into second gear to come up.'

No, I was certainly not so silly as to think my love, and you could say knowledge, of this part of the country had a claim on him as a fellow countryman. Of course not. And yet ...

'There used to be a big tree just there.' I pointed to a hundred yards or so down the front of the hill.

'There was no tree there,' said the man, swaying and leaning. 'There was never any tree.'

'We used to call it the *mawonga* tree.'

'It is the wrong name,' said the drunk.

Interesting, watching history being unmade, the past forsworn.

A little way down the side of the hill a few black women were listening and they were curious. They were probably, too, pleased at this little excitement in what must have been poor and uneventful lives.

Some yards away was the bungalow someone had built. From the windows peered black children's faces.

Not asking his permission, since he would not have given it, we walked to where we could see the crowded windows. Suddenly, no children. I stood, peering in. The windows were shut, on a hot afternoon. Inside a dozen or so children were immured. They stood shyly together in the centre of the room. Just children, of all ages. Not a toy, piece of paper, exercise book, any kind of book; nothing for them to play with or use their minds on. Where was the nearest school? Banket. Unless there was a farm school somewhere.

This was before Mugabe licensed the grabbing of the white farms.

It hurt, seeing that house, and the children without any kind of – well, anything. Nothing. It was a way of making sure children were safe and out of mischief. Lock them up in an empty house …

It hurts now. Give us education, give us books, give us exercise books – such is the cry, but perhaps not so much now, when there is so little food to go round, so little of anything. By now those children will be out-of-work adults.

They might easily be dead, from Aids, or hunger.

Long ago, in 1956, I was in Cold Comfort Farm, a 'progressive' farm that gave education to children and adolescents before the black government came. There I met an idealistic young man, planning to be a teacher, who said he wanted to be educated so as to help his people, 'to give my life for my people'.

Idealistic youngsters don't necessarily turn out well.

That idealistic youngster soon became Didymus Mutasa, a bosom crony of Mugabe. Not long ago he said it wouldn't matter if so many people died of Aids or of anything else. 'We would be better off with two million people less,' said this man who has become one of the most corrupt, most unscrupulous black leaders in Africa.

I wonder, did someone cut down the old *mawonga* tree? Was it really old? Did it fall down? These trees are studded among the lower-growing trees of the highveld; they are taller than the other trees, whitish-trunked, and their boughs do not grow flattish and layered like the *musasas*.

Our tree was a sort of a landmark. It was always full of birds. Once a swarm of locusts came down from the north, settled on every tree, and loaded a branch of the *mawonga*. It broke under the weight.

Bees lived in the tree. You could see the hole, from yards away, with the insects buzzing about. At intervals, a group of men came up from the fields and made a smoking fire at the right place under the bees. When the bees, noticing the smoke, began to buzz and fuss and also to fall dazed, the men leaned a naked tree trunk against the *mawonga* trunk and one clambered up. At the level of the hole he inserted his arm, brought out shards and combs of honey, which were put into a paraffin tin. He brushed off bees but did not seem much discommoded. Then he came sliding down. A basin full of honey, combs, bee bread were for us, for the house, but a couple of big tins went down to the compound.

It must have been a large colony. They swarmed quite often. We would hear the swelling drone as the departing swarm passed over the house and away to find a place to make their new hives.

Of that tree my parents said: 'We'll never get off the farm, and they'll bury us under the *mawonga* tree.'

'Well, that old tree will still be here when we are gone.'

As it happened, it lasted not much longer than they did.

The swallows, when they came, at about the start of the rainy season, swirled about the front of the house, and around the lower part of the *mawonga* tree.

And when the swallows left, in April or May, my mother would mourn, 'Oh, the swallows will be in England soon. They'll get there before us. Can you imagine them dipping over the ponds? When the swallows came in spring you'd know summer would soon be here …'

'I wish the rains would come properly,' says my father. 'Just look at those clouds. There's not a drop of rain in the lot of them.'

'They wouldn't be here if it wasn't going to rain soon,' says my mother. 'No rain, no insects, no swallows.'

The name *'mawonga'* is Shona, how it sounds. Names for this tree are *Pericopsis* and *Angolensis*.

Provisions

Two small children were at the table, which was inside the windows that were 'just like the bow of a ship!' so said my mother. There was a proper little commotion of a scene going on. The little girl was wailing that she wouldn't eat her egg, and the boy echoed that he wouldn't either. 'I don't like slimy eggs,' said the girl.

At which Daddy snaps, 'What a damned disgrace. You won't eat your eggs. Think of the starving little children in India.'

These starving Indian children had a role in our family meals, and later I discovered that their fate was regularly appealed to when middle-class children disliked their fare.

'Think of the starving Indian children' was bound to get a laugh at school, for instance.

Why didn't my father say, Think of the hungry children in the compound? But he never did. Deprivation has had to be a long way off to be effective. And I don't think the children in the compound were starving or went hungry. The compound was for the farm labourers and we were supposed to know how many were there. That is because by law a farmer had to provide rations, mealie-meal – the staple food – peanuts, beans, weighed out once a week, the boss-boy supervising. All the labourers in this district were from Nyasaland: this area was on the path southwards for the men, and some women, who walked south, for days stopping at this farm or that. They stopped where there were relatives, or the boss-boy was a relative. Thus my father might joke, 'We may think we are in control but don't you believe it. The boss-boys are.' Now, if a party of Nyasalanders went through the compound some stayed, if there was a chance of work. Then there were a good many more on the farm than was officially the case. That meant the rations would be stretched. That meant some children might be hungry.

'Damn it, Smoke,' my father would expostulate. 'You tell me there are twenty-five in the compound, and I've provided twenty-five rations. But you are asking for more.'

'Yes, Baas. My brother came last night and he has his wife with him.'

'Am I employing him?'

'No, Baas, but he will look for work next week.'

These 'brothers' caused instant and inevitable misunderstanding, for every relative designated a 'brother' was owed hospitality.

'And so, how many children?'

At which old Smoke (because he smoked *dagga* hemp) was evasive and mumbled, 'Not very many.'

'But there aren't meant to be children in the compound.'

'No, Baas.'

'So how many people are really living down there?' my father could have asked, but did not, because then old Smoke would have had to lie.

But for the evening of the day their rations were given out old Smoke had the keys to the storeroom.

So, if there were no starving children in our compound I am sure none had boiled eggs and toast and butter, let alone marmalade and jam.

In April 2007, the BBC ran a series about Edwardian food. 'This is what our grandparents ate.' Impossible: so far has our diet evolved away from those imposing heavy meals. But the food on our table was impressive enough, and when I escaped from it, as food became lighter and healthier, I would look back and marvel.

Breakfast: various kinds of porridge and the new corn-flakes, then bacon and eggs and sausages, with tomatoes and the delicious fried bread, which is no longer the same now that beef dripping has become obsolete. Toast, butter, mar-malade. Then there was morning tea, with biscuits and scones. Lunch was cold meat, various kinds of potatoes, or made-up dishes, like cauliflower cheese or macaroni. Then pudding. Afternoon tea, with more scones, biscuits, and cake. We chil-dren had supper, and plenty of it – too much – and the starv-ing Indian children often played their part. Dinner, when we got older, was a proper meal, with roasts, chops, liver, kidneys, tongue, and wonderful vegetables from my mother's vegetable garden. And puddings.

This amazing diet was going on through the seventies, the eighties ... At my brother's lunch table there it all was, at my son John's. And, yes, they did both die of heart-attacks but surely one has to ask, how did they survive so long?

When I remonstrated with my brother about meals that would fuel a labourer, a navvy, he replied, 'But we have to keep up our standards.'

In other words, it was eating that said, 'Look what I can afford to eat.' This was true everywhere in the legacies of the British Empire. And we may hear Australians even now laugh helplessly, describing Christmas meals that Dickens would have recognized, including the pudding, and mince pies, with the thermometer at ninety. I don't know how often I watched my father saying, 'Oh, God, do we have to have a Christmas dinner? I want to plant out the tobacco seedlings – replant the mealies – make the silage.' And that scene went on (does it still?) on 25 December because standards had to be kept up.

The heavy Edwardian meals went on in our house at least until the early thirties. But new ideas were brewing, and the parents succumbed to a hundred diets and fancies, some of them like those that are around today. In our household *Nature* magazine came in with the *Observer* and the news-letters about English politics. We knew about roughage, vitamins, cooking vegetables the right way. I was sent to visit friends of my parents for a fortnight and was overthrown by encountering the opposite of everything my parents then believed. 'Meat!' insisted my hostess. 'It's the only thing. And you are a growing girl – meat.' If I put forward the latest

theories from home – the necessity of salads, steaming vegetables – I was overthrown by burning convictions absolutely
opposite to those of my parents. This happened more than
once. I had hardly reached my teens when I was in possession
of all the latest fads of the time. I have in my lifetime seen
every commodity lauded as essential, or despised as *bad* –
sugar has always been Very Bad Indeed.

Now, this preoccupation with health in our house did not
prevent my father getting diabetes, or my mother complaining of a hundred ills. Meanwhile, her need to stuff me with
food made me miserable, because I was getting fat. Yes,
nothing has changed. While I was not subject to the awful
girlie magazines with their prescriptions, I and the girls I
knew did not want to get fat. I devised a diet for myself, which
impresses me because of its determination that I would not
succumb to malnutrition. For three or four months I ate
tomatoes and peanut butter, thinking that between them they
would give me adequate vitamins. It worked. I lost weight
while my mother wept and bewailed, but that also because I
was acquiring my adult figure, which wasn't bad at all, and
which she hated.

If there was ever a woman who would have been happy to
see her little daughter never leave fairy childhood behind,
then it was my mother. I started to make myself dresses, I
earned money, and throughout this process she exhorted,
complained, warned of all kinds of disastrous ends for me.

I recommend this diet, tomatoes and peanut butter, to
slimmers, but I don't know what the experts would say. Of

course, tomatoes just in out of the hot sun, peanut butter made from fresh peanuts, just out of the ground, yes, these are not easily got, and certainly not in London, with all its piled plenty.

And what of my father, while I refused to eat, except my chosen two foodstuffs? He was too ill, he was so dreadfully ill, but now might easily have said, 'Think of the hungry children in Britain,' for the Slump had set in. The swathes of the working class ate bread and marge sprinkled with sugar, or bread and dripping, drank strong tea heaped with sugar. Soon I was to meet RAF men, when the war came, whose childhoods had been like this, or similar. 'How about the hungry children [June 2007] in Darfur, in the Congo, in ... Zimbabwe, in ...'

Sometimes it is asked, rhetorically enough, 'What will our descendants blame us for as we now blame the slave traders?' Surely that is easy enough. They will say that one half of the world stuffed itself with food while the other half was hungry. Easy to imagine some prime minister, hoping for a good mark from history, apologizing for the disgusting greed of us, his forebears.

I do not see how there can be forgiveness of what we are doing.

Probably the most disgusting sight in the world is to watch plates carried out of an American restaurant, still piled with food, and see the garbage bins in the street piled high with uneaten food. As disgusting as seeing the same in England, food that would feed thousands of hungry people. Hungry and dying. They die, they are dying as I write this ...

Well, would you forgive it? I doubt it.

But while children in Britain, not to mention parts of Europe, were going without, here in old Southern Rhodesia the food was better than anything you can get now. The vegetables were grown without pesticides and artificial fertilizers. The meat had never heard of hormones. Chickens had a healthy life: no one had heard of battery chickens. And what very good use was being made, on the farms, of what was grown. Some of those concocted dishes have disappeared from memory, I think. For instance, all the different dishes made from what we call sweetcorn, the fresh maize kernels, the cobs just brought up from the fields.

The mealie kernels in a cheese sauce, baked so it had a slight crust, or cooked in batter, similarly with a crust, all kinds of soups and stews. There was a sort of vegetable stew consisting of maize, pieces of pumpkin, onions, beans, potatoes, with or without a little meat, according to the vagaries of the new diet rules. When I went to Argentina, we asked the driver allotted us to let us eat where he did, in the restaurants for the locals. And there I encountered this stew again, but it had chilli in it and tomatoes. And now we come to the pumpkin, which no one seems able to cook in Britain. Pieces of pumpkin are sprinkled with sugar and cinnamon and allowed to caramelize. Delicious, particularly with roast meat. Or pumpkin fried with onion, or mashed with cinnamon and nutmeg. Pumpkin soups. And, best of all, pumpkin batter fritters, crisp and spicy.

Meanwhile my mother was trying to get the labourers to

eat the vegetables she was growing so successfully. They liked the spinach, they liked onions. But while she explained about vitamins (yes, she did – 'They have to know sometime, don't they?'), they would not eat tomatoes. No, they would not, not then. She begged them to go to the vegetable garden and the garden boy would give them all the tomatoes they wanted. Or runner beans. 'But cabbage is so good for them,' she might wail. But not cabbage, not then. All that has changed. They took mealies from the fields, with or without permission, and a band of Nyasers passing through could strip a line of them. 'Well, what do you expect?' said my father. 'Wouldn't you?'

'But it's thieving,' she protested. 'What else would you call it?'

'Well, old thing, I would say that is the right word for it, yes.'

I haven't mentioned the fruits we took for granted. Grenadilla vines grew wild in some parts of the country. Guava trees were in many gardens. Pawpaw trees – the big pawpaws were everywhere. So were avocados. Plantains did well, but not bananas. In more than one of the houses I lived in, lychees grew outside the kitchen door. Oranges, lemons, grapefruit: the old Southern Rhodesia grew everything, somewhere, and I haven't mentioned the peaches, or the mangoes, from Mutare, or …

In short, the diet enjoyed by the whites, and some of the better-off blacks, could not be bought now for money or for love. It doesn't exist.

Provisions – in Town

The day starts early, with breakfast at seven: the offices open at eight. The meal is the full English breakfast. The men having departed, the women begin their day. If there are babies or small children, they will have to be kept pacified until the important business of the order books is complete. The delivery men arrive on bicycles, which they leave leaning against trees or gates, and they take the books through to the kitchen where the cook checks them and makes notes. Whichever arrives first he takes to the missus – 'Madam' was a later embellishment.

The cook, whose real name isn't used in this household, probably Isaac, or Joshua, or some resounding biblical name, says, 'Missus, here is the fruit and veg.' Each delivery boy has a little exercise book with the number of the house on it – let us say 183 Livingstone Avenue. Each page is dated; there is a stub of pencil attached by string to the little book.

The lady of the house looks at yesterday's order. Cook has ticked each item to say it arrived.

She knows she must make sure there are plenty of onions,

tomatoes, and something in the line of spinach. These are for the 'boys' – the servants. In Southern Rhodesia all the house servants were male, whereas in South Africa they were and are female. Why? Who can say, by now?

She writes,

2 lbs potatoes
4 lbs onions
4 lbs spinach
1 pawpaw
6 plantains
6 oranges

She says to the man who is waiting and watching her, 'I've put spinach and onion. What else?' Meaning, what else do *you* want? Fruit, at this stage of the colony's development, was not what the servants wanted.

'Pumpkin, missus.' She adds, '1 pumpkin'.

'Grenadillas,' says the man.

'Fruit salad for tonight.' She writes, '3 lbs grenadillas'.

'That's all,' says Moses, or Benjamin, or Jacob. He puts another little book before her. This is the grocery book, and there can be, usually is, a little tussle over this order, amiable or not, according to mood.

She looks at yesterday's order. Each item ticked.

'Rice, missus,' says the man.

She says, 'But we had five pounds of rice yesterday.'

'We need rice, missus,' he insists. And adds, 'You had rice and stew, missus.'

'Very well,' she says, and writes, '5 lbs rice'.

'Curry powder.'

Now, the servants adore curry powder, which they might even sprinkle on their mealie-meal porridge – the *sadza*.

She looks quizzical, but puts down, '1 tin curry powder'.

'Sugar,' he says.

And now here is a real little bone for them to chew over.

Never is there enough sugar. This man will provide food for any of his friends who drop in, his 'brothers', and probably his friends' friends.

Sacks of mealie-meal stand in the pantry, with sacks of beans and peanuts. But the sugar sack is always mysteriously getting thinner and lower.

She says, 'We had a ten-pound sack of sugar last week.'

'Sugar, missus,' he says softly, and she writes, '10 lbs sugar'. One by one, jams, honey, coffee, tea are added and then that is done, the grocery book, and here is the little book that carries such a charge. This is the butcher's book.

I returned to Southern Rhodesia less than ten years after I left it and was immediately surprised by the amount of meat. Every fridge was stacked with it, including the vegetable trays. 'We couldn't have eaten all that meat,' I cried. 'Impossible!' But we did.

And all the servants loved meat, *nyama*, and wanted more.

Yesterday's order read:

5 lbs best beef for roasting
2 lbs liver
2 lbs bacon
2 lbs rump steak

Now, the liver from yesterday's lunch was only half eaten.

She ought to ask, 'What happened to the leftover liver?'

She doesn't.

She and her husband would eat the roast tonight. There was a lot of the stew left over from last night.

'Ah, how was the stew?' she attempts to jest, knowing better than to ask, 'I wonder how many people helped you eat it.'

'The stew was very nice, missus,' he says promptly. 'Do you remember? You and the Baas said it was a good stew.'

'And so it was.'

She writes:

2 lbs ox kidney
3 lbs mince
2 chickens

Chickens were then not an everyday meal, but eaten on special occasions: she plans a Sunday lunch party.

'And we'll have another roast on Sunday too,' she says.

She would like to order brains, but this man's tribal customs do not permit him to cook brains and certainly not to eat them.

Shoulder of pork

4 lbs sausages

And now she orders the meat for them, 'the boys': '4 lbs boys' meat'. This meant all kinds of scraps and bits and bones. Much later I ate 'boys'' meat, cooked by a clearly star cook. The little bits of this and that and bones, cooked in a thin tin-can type of container, with some onions, were utterly delicious. '3 lbs soup meat': more scraps and bones, and the servants had most of this. '3 lbs dogs' meat.' This was more bone than meat: big bones lay about on the lawns and had to be cleared away.

From time to time complaints were made by the 'boys' that the dogs' meat was better than theirs. They resented the dogs and their privileged status.

'And now what else?' asks the lady of the house, thinking how sad that this colony's lamb was not worth eating.

'Tongue?' suggests the man.

They all liked tongue.

'That butcher's brawn is very good,' he says.

'3 lbs brawn', she writes. Neither she nor her husband likes it, but why not?

'If you order a piece of ham I can make pea and ham soup,' he says. He claps his hand on his knee, to show which bit of pig she should order.

She writes, 'knuckle of ham', and hands the book back to him.

He glances over it to make sure all is there.

She tells her husband that she enjoys 'sparring' with Joshua
– or whoever.

'Provided you understand he is taking advantage of you,'
says the master of the house and the wage-earner, establishing
his authority.

'Oh, go on, what does it all amount to?'

'Quite a lot if you ever add it together.'

Outside the three delivery boys are on their bicycles, each
leaning with a foot on the veranda. The cook throws the little
books, one, two, three – neatly caught – and off they cycle,
down to the shops, which are no more than a mile or so away.

Done, she thinks. Everybody's fed – I hope.

And now is the time for the children, or if she has none,
soon she will go off to a morning tea party at the house of
another wife, where there will be scones, biscuits, cake, a
whole range of goodies, the achievement of this household's
cook.

When the girls exchange recipes, they are for cakes and
puddings; meat can and does look after itself. They might
mourn that there should be another animal invented: 'Beef,
beef, beef, – sometimes I think I'll be a vegetarian.'

My Brother Harry Tayler

It was the early days of the Second World War: British battleships were in the Pacific Ocean on their warlike pursuits. They were the *Repulse* and the *Prince of Wales*. Both were unsinkable. Just like the *Titanic*. Is it permissible for ratepayers and concerned citizens to wonder about the later fate of the 'experts' who have such untrue ideas about the capacities of the big ships? Do they become knights and lords? Are they transferred to other committees to pronounce on the viability of shipping?

My brother was on the *Repulse*. The Japanese sank both ships in twenty minutes. When the news came through it stunned us. Those hundreds and hundreds of men drowned … but more definite news took longer. Where was it to come from? War correspondents were not yet roving the Pacific. Then survivors told their stories and slowly it all came out. My brother wrote a letter, which did not arrive at once. He was not one of the world's letter-writers, my brother.

'It wasn't a very nice experience,' he admitted. On that dreadful morning, when the bombs hit, he was standing by a companionway going up to a deck while men were hastening past him, when someone said, 'Are you going up, Tayler?' Thus propelled, he went up the ladder, and found the ship already sinking. He walked down a slanting deck into the sea, and swam away with a swarm of survivors. He was far enough away when the *Repulse* went down. He was in the water for some hours, surrounded by corpses, oil, wreckage, and the sharks were around but were put off, probably, by the oil. Then a British ship picked them up and took them to Ceylon. There they told their tales to reporters, and were allowed to recuperate. Harry was assigned to the *Aurora* where he spent the rest of the war, in the Mediterranean. There he went pretty deaf, from gunfire – more than he had been: he was going deaf even in his teens.

I met him in Cape Town. It happened like this.

My first child, John Wisdom, was never one to put up uncomplainingly with difficulties and annoyances. The birth of my second child, his sister, shocked him. Never in my life have I heard such howls of rage, betrayal, when he realized that this new creature, this baby, was here to stay. He attacked the baby, but also attacked me, pummelling me with already savage little fists. 'Why have you done this – to *me*?' was the message.

Consultations. I was a bit frazzled myself. While I have heard many a man say something like 'My grandmother had eight children in eight years and was never a day the worse for it', it is my belief that having babies too fast takes it out of women. A woman who lived in the next house begged to be allowed to look after the little girl: she had wanted girl children, and did not get them. I would take John right away to the coast where he would have his mother to himself, day and night, and recover.

I have written about the journey to Cape Town, five days in a coupé the size of a small pony box. Sometimes veterans of life may be observed looking back over the years and wondering which of their experiences was the worst. I aver that being shut up with a hyperactive small boy for five days in a small space comes pretty high on a list of unlikeable experiences. But, then, there was the sea at last and the hotel. It was on the front at Sea Point, and the hotels along there were dedicated to pleasure, signalled by the strings of coloured fairy-lights each wore on its front. The hotel was crammed. The survivors from the Fall of Singapore had just arrived. There was every kind of traveller caught by the war, forced into accommodation much worse, it was easy to guess, than most were used to. There were all kinds of official, bureaucrat, clerk, lacking their own quarters, which were probably requisitioned for the war effort.

Among them were some Quakers and to them I owe a conversation I needed badly. While it could not be said that I found the Southern Rhodesian regime attractive, I had never heard anyone describe it without prejudice. It must be remembered that in 1924, the year my parents arrived in the colony, there had just been a plebiscite or some kind of vote taken about whether this new land wanted to be South Africa's sixth province or not. All the Rhodesians voted, 'No, we shall be a British self-governing colony.'

The Quakers, half a dozen officials, hearing that I was from 'that obstinate little country', started discussing it. Much to my advantage.

'Really ... there could be nothing more ridiculous. They are going it alone, so they say. There are a hundred thousand whites governing half a million natives [the then correct word for the blacks]. But every time we – South Africans – pass a law, they copy it and pass the same law. They copy each one of our Land Laws. So why not stay a part of South Africa? Have you ever visited there? British this, British that, it makes you sick ...' And so on. This made me think, as they say, to good purpose.

This over-full, noisy hotel pleased John and, above all, there was no baby sister. He had a very good time. To the veranda of this hotel one day came Midshipman Harry Tayler, an amazingly good-looking young man, who had every woman in the place peering at him through the windows or making excuses to take tea on the veranda, so as to watch him.

And now I could hear what had happened with the *Repulse*.

'You see,' said my brother, 'I think I got a bit of a shock. I only realized that afterwards. I was in a bit of a daze, for weeks. Ceylon is a blur, you see.'

'How long were you in the sea, waiting to be picked up?'

'I don't know. They tell me it was hours. It seemed like days. The water was warm – that wasn't a bother. But there were a lot of dead people floating about. And I had known some of them. The sun was too hot. It was burning me. I had blisters from the sun. I tried to keep my head wet. There were other people hanging on to anything that floated, and calling out for help. I saw a report in *The Times*, I think, from one of the other survivors. He said there were sharks. I didn't see any. What self-respecting shark would want to be in that oil? But when you come to think of it, I suppose the oil was quite a help with the sunburn.'

'Do you ever think about the man who told you to go up the companionway to the deck?'

'Yes, that was lucky, if you like. I only just got up to the deck and swam away before the whole ship went down. I would have gone with it. But you see, Tigs [my childhood name], you can't really take it in. Not something as enormous as that.'

'Do you think about it?'

'Not if I can help it. It simply wasn't very nice, any of it.'

And now imagine this conversation going on, but it was decades later – the sequel. Harry, who had gone through the war in the Mediterranean, was treated for his deafness in London, but he didn't get a really good hearing-aid until he was old. He married, had children, had jobs all to do with his amazing knowledge of the bush, the veld, the animals, the plants, and then the blacks won their war and were the government, and Harry said he couldn't live under a black government, and he went down to South Africa, before there was a black government there too and then, much too young, he got a heart-attack and died. Meanwhile we met, several

times, in my kitchen in London. During those years we had
not been good friends. He supported the whites in the war,
and I was on the side of the blacks. So when we met, both old
now, there was a great deal to tell each other. When we could.
We had so little in common, my brother and I, that it was
often hard to find subjects to talk about. I took it for granted
that I had to keep quiet, keep my mouth shut, when he began
spouting the stock platitudes about the inferiority of the
blacks, and he often looked tolerant, meaning that my views
on this and that were uncomfortable to him.

But then, not so long before he died, he said he had something to tell me. He wanted me to understand something. His
wife had died by then, of a heart-attack, and he was lonely. He
was suffering that need of the old: he needed to explain
something before it was too late. Tell somebody, anybody, as if
what he had to tell could have no reality unless it was in
somebody else's mind too.

During the Liberation War, my brother was not a combat-
ant because he was too old, but the farmers too old for actual
fighting were out most nights in lorries or armoured cars,
keeping in touch with the white farms by radio or dropping in
to see if everyone was all right. There were ambushes on the
roads: the freedom-fighters might mine them, it was dan-
gerous, though not as bad as actually being in the army, and
Harry, like all those men, thoroughly enjoyed it.

When pacifists, or people trying to limit war, decide to
forget that some men thoroughly enjoy war, they are making
a bad mistake.

My son John, that once-belligerent little boy, loved war. He adored crawling through the bush, armed to the teeth, in great danger.

Three times now I have heard men talking over past happy times with the men they were fighting. They have everything in common.

One was my father, who used to visit a German small-mine worker (a small-mine worker was put down a trench, or a shaft, for the sake of a few pennyweight of gold, for as long as a chancy seam lasted). German and English ex-servicemen: they had been in the Trenches at the same time in the same area. They would discuss for hours how they were on this patrol or that, were nearly wounded – before they actually were – discuss the competence or otherwise of their officers.

The roads were rutted and had potholes. Jolting around in old lorries was the worst part of those nightly sorties. One night the lorry Harry was on, with other men at the back, crowded together, went into a rut or hit a boulder and Harry had a bad jar, all over his body, but there was a blow to his head, which smashed against the back of the cabin.

'That was a really bad bash, and I felt so peculiar. I rang the doc – you know, with petrol rationing you didn't use the car unless you had to – and I told him how I felt and he said, "No, that's not concussion, you don't sound concussed to me." But I felt so … I don't know how to tell you. Do you remember malaria?'

'No, I don't.'

'Well, one minute you're shivering and shaking and the next you've never felt so clear and on top of everything. But, no, it wasn't that, and I had no temperature or anything. I wasn't ill. I felt I must be mad, everything was so bright and clear, and it took me days to understand. Then I did, quite suddenly. This was what I was like before the *Repulse*. That blow on the head had sent me back to normal. I was suddenly my real self, you see. I was suddenly myself. I had to face the fact that I'd spent years of my life, getting on for forty, not myself at all. It was as if I was behind a glass wall. Oh, I don't think I can explain it …'

'You're doing pretty well, Harry. Go on.'

'That means Monica [his wife] never knew me as myself, not my real self, when everything is sharp and clear. And my children – it's so hard to come to terms with, Tigs. There was something about the *Repulse* thing that sent me off centre … Well, could *you* tell all those years how I was?'

'We haven't been seeing much of each other, have we?'

'No, I suppose not.'

And to reply to what he was asking, I had thought that my brother was rather slow, but had put that down to his being so deaf. And now he said it himself.

'I thought perhaps it was that I had been so deaf – I didn't have a real hearing-aid. But it wasn't that. I might have been deaf but I could see everything. I had my senses. But everything was dulled. Muffled. Like being under water and hearing sounds coming from a distance. You see, Tigs, it's most of my life: I simply haven't been here at all.'

Getting-off-the-Farm

In the middle of the war my parents moved into town – to Salisbury, now Harare. It was impossible to nurse my father any longer on the farm. But the old house, leaking so badly a storm was marked by rain pattering on the linoleum, and where the four winds blew, and sometimes inside as well as outside, had suited him better than the bungalow, which he hated.

The diabetes was very bad. They had not refined the treatment then, the doctors, and looking at his illness from its beginning to its end, the constant theme was the restriction of food, and his diet was so limited that my image of him is this haunted, gaunt man, sitting at the table with, beside him, little brass scales, where he measured an ounce of this, two ounces of that, half a scone, a little potato. Everything has changed: now the doctors are so clever and flexible, balancing insulin against the food, so that living with a diabetic, it is easy to forget that he is one. If my father's doctors had had these levels of skill he would not have been so dreadfully ill.

Fate, or my *karma*, or chance, has caused me to have to look after a diabetic, just as my mother did, and I can compare what happens now with then. How lucky we are in our medicines: diabetic sufferers have no idea how they would have been dealt with not so long ago.

We are all conditioned, wired, evolved, to accept calamity as a blow, a suddenness. He fell off a horse; an arrow pierced his eye; she died in childbirth, of a burst appendix, of food-poisoning; there was a sniper, a suicide-bomber, a rock fall; or a fire, a flood, a car crash. But to imagine, let alone describe, a slow, long descent through illness is hard. If I say my mother nursed my father day and night for the last four years of his illness, a minute-by-minute vigilance, while his organs failed, one by one, and everything went, until he was begging to be given death, then it is hard to take in. And she had nursed him for the ten years before that.

She didn't have enough help. I and others would look after my father for an afternoon, an evening, so she could go out, but she really needed people who would say, 'I'll take over for the weekend so that you can ...' very probably just sleep. I didn't know how to cope with that apparatus of syringes and test-tubes, and the batteries of pills, among which there was not one for his dreadful depression.

It was such a bad time for everyone, the war and its aftermath, but particularly for my mother. We now know the war did have an end – 1939–45 – but while it dragged on, we didn't know, and no one foresaw the awfulness of the after-war years. It is so hard to convey the unremittingness of it all, the deadening slog. While they were going on, my father's last years, it was hard to feel, with my mother, what it was really like for her, but I would say that people who have had to do something of the same kind themselves will understand.

His children, certainly, were no joy for my father. My brother nearly went down with the *Repulse,* but was saved, and then he had a long, hard war in the Mediterranean, where so much fighting went on. As for his daughter, I left a husband and two children and married a German, classed as an enemy alien. My parents were not anti-German, but there are stereotypes of German. One is the large, hearty, probably pipe-smoking, good-natured man, rather like Father Christmas, whom they would have liked. Another is the Prussian, aloof, correct, cold, ungiving. How could they have liked my second husband? And he was a Communist, a real one (and stayed one until he died). There were whole hinterlands here that luckily they knew nothing about: for instance, that Gottfried only married me, as enemy aliens married local girls when they could, to keep himself out of the internment camp. But it must have been obvious to them, particularly to my father, that Gottfried and I were not well suited. As it is put. Gottfried, hating everything about his life in Southern Rhodesia, was inverately polite, and they were polite too. Now I cannot see how the behaviour of my father's daughter could have been worse for him.

But he and I understood each other very well. When I sat with him on those long afternoons and evenings, he would hold my hand and we were complicit in a rage of under-standing. I think my father's rage at the Trenches took me over, when I was very young, and has never left me. Do children feel their parents' emotions? Yes, we do, and it is a legacy I could have done without. What is the use of it? It is as if that old war is in my own memory, my own consciousness.

My father dreamed a lot about the Trenches, and my mother said that sometimes she felt as if his old comrades were there in the room with him – with us.

'They were such good chaps,' my father would say, 'such fine men. And they all died in Passchendaele. Every one of my company. And I would have died with them, but I got the shrapnel in my leg just before the battle. I must have told you – I'm sure I did. But those fine chaps, they would be alive now. They were just cannon fodder, that's all.'

Years later, in London, I visited the Imperial War Museum, where they have created a most uncomfortably realistic set of Trenches. Standing looking at them was a woman, and she was crying. I saw she was crying with rage so I went to stand by her. She gave me a glance and took in that I was at one with her. 'It's as if they were just rubbish,' she said. 'Like rubbish, to be shovelled into the Trenches. They weren't worth anything, you see.' Exactly.

And my father talked more and more about cannon fodder. 'If you had only known them,' he said, holding my hand hard. 'Such good men. I keep thinking of them.' And my father, crying, an old man's tears, his eyes wide and childlike – an old man's eyes (but he not yet sixty) – and he was murmuring the names of those fine chaps, his men, who died in the mud at Passchendaele, while the wireless, which was never turned off, told us news from the battlefronts in Europe and in the Pacific.

'I think of them, yes, I do, there's never a day I don't think of them, oh, such fine young chaps …'

My mother might come in and sit on the old basket armchair, brought from the farm – her chair. She was utterly worn out. I could see she wanted to get a few minutes' nap, perhaps, and she rested her hand on her cheek, the hand where the rings were loose on her fingers.

'I must have told you,' my father said, seeing her sitting there, 'yes, I'm sure I did. If the shrapnel hadn't got me I would have died with them, and sometimes I wonder if it wouldn't have been better if I had.

'The thing is,' said my father, rousing himself, 'I keep thinking, it could all have been done better. Done differently, don't you see? Emily? Emily?'

'Let her sleep,' I begged. 'She's so tired.'

'Emily?' he shouted, in a panic.

'Here I am,' said my mother, returning.

In the District there were other soldiers from the Great War, the war to end all war. One woman had lost a husband and three sons to the Trenches; she had one son left, too young for the war. She would say, dignified with her sorrow, that when she looked at this youngest son, she saw all her other dead soldiers. When those survivors of the First World War met, they would talk in a way that has fallen out of fashion. 'The armament-makers,' they would say, 'they made the war happen. Krupps made our war.' The German small-mine worker down the hill, my father's friend, who had bits of shrapnel in him too, from the German Trenches, talked about the armament-makers, Krupps and the profiteers.

How strange that the words – and the idea – have dropped out of our minds. The 'military industrial complex' does not have the same ring, does not remind us, or make us think. When a war starts up in Africa, a pointless war, apparently, for the sake of a few acres of scrub, my parents, that generation, would have said, 'It's the armament-makers at it again. It's the profiteers.' And what has been achieved at the end of it? A few hundred dead, but millions of pounds, spent on weapons, safely lodged in somebody's pockets.

Grocz's pictures were of the profiteers and armament-makers, who did well out of that war.

Profiteers and armament-makers – gone from our speech and, so it seems, from our minds.

At the funeral I was too angry to listen or watch. My eyes were shut, and I was praying, if curses can be called a prayer.

My mother was exhausted and she did not quickly get over it

And so, that was that.

Servant Problems

All over the world, from every village, every little shanty, people stream to the towns. This was true in old Southern Rhodesia, and it is true in Zimbabwe. It seems everyone agrees with Lenin and his 'the idiocy of village life'. Oh, lovely towns, full of excitements and opportunities. But people are not always welcome in towns. In Salisbury, for instance, or in any Southern Rhodesian town, the blacks were only allowed to stay if they had a job. This was the same policy as the infamous 'apartheid' of South Africa. 'If you are useful to the whites, then stay. Otherwise, back you go to your rural huts.' And what did they find in towns? In Salisbury, every white house had, as well as a lavatory like a sentry box, emptied by the sanitary carts once a week, servants' quarters, or 'kias' (short for what? I don't know), a low, small brick room or two, just off the sanitary lane. They were supposed to house the 'boys' working for that house but always held many more. So what did they find in the way of excitements and general blessings in, let's say, Salisbury?

I think there were films, and I certainly remember that

there were dance-halls. What they found there at the back of the white man's house, in the brick rooms, was each other. The company was noisy, funny, full of laughter and gossip. I once wrote a story called 'A Home for the Highland Cattle', after spending hours watching from back windows the dramas of the 'boys' lives, where a woodpile, shrubs, a cooking fire were props for a never-ending drama. At least until the Second World War most houses might have as many as five servants. The cookboy had enough to do, but the houseboy might finish cleaning the rooms by mid-morning. There might be two houseboys, and a gardener, hardly overworked, and a 'piccanin' for odd jobs. They were paid a minimum wage, were fed rations, and the white family's cast-offs were worn often in ways not envisaged by the makers. I do not remember any ambitious servants. Once, a lively and clever young man, our general servant, was begged by us – Gottfried Lessing and me – to go to night classes to learn book-keeping, anything, paid for by us, of course: he refused, saying he liked dancing too much.

All day, every day, men from their villages went from house to house begging for work. If they found a position, the joys of the towns were theirs. Otherwise out you go, and the police were always after them.

In the war, when Salisbury was crammed, was over-full, Gottfried Lessing and I found a place to live – temporary, like everything in those days. It was a very large room, with a passage on two sides, leading nowhere. Into these spaces went a wardrobe and chest of drawers and a marble slab that held hot-plates, a kettle and a sink. There was a bathroom. The arrival of the baby made little work. He was a good baby, as they say, and I did know that there could be other kinds of babe, because my first, John, was far from good. But this one slept, and was amiable. To wash his nappies took half an hour, and they dried out in the sun in a couple of hours. I and Gottfried decided that we didn't need a servant. What for? He would be more trouble than a convenience.

Now, in the avenues where the houses were, men begging for work came round all day, to be dealt with by the cook and the 'boys' who saw them as competitors and didn't want them. But the word went around at once that there was this missus in such-and-such a house and she needed a 'boy'. Several times a day there was a knock on the door and the pleading, 'I want work, missus'; 'Please give me work, missus'; even, 'You can teach me to cook, I learn well.' And so on. I wrote out a large notice and tacked it to my outer door: 'Do Not Ask for Work Here. There Is No Work.'

My mother was appalled. She had plenty of time for me now my father had gone. 'What will the neighbours say?' There were eight rooms like ours in this block, and there was a 'boy' for each. These servants had to find accommodation in the 'location', which meant them coming in every morning and leaving in the evening in time to beat the curfew at eight o'clock.

What did they find to do? They loitered about the streets or found some friendly house where they did not mind them hanging around at the back.

'Mother, tell me, just what is this man going to find to do? Just look, take a look. I suppose he could push the baby out for a walk.'

'Oh, no, no, that would be very wrong. It would be asking for trouble.'

'What trouble?' I said.

'Then I'll just clean up a bit for you.'

'No. Stop it. *No.*'

She desisted.

'Then I'll just take off Gottfried's shirts and get them washed.'

'No. There are laundries. Leave them. *No.*'

Next her servant arrived to beg me to employ his brother, a relative. He badly wanted to live in Salisbury, could not find work, but if I employed him …

'For one thing it would mean his coming in every morning and going back every evening. And you are at least three miles out.'

The plan was for this man to live with him, in my mother's servants' quarters.

'It would be all right. He can walk. Or you can buy him a bicycle, and he can ride, only half an hour.'

'I don't need a servant. Can't you see?'

'Yes, you do. He will clean it nice-nice, he's a good boy, missus.'

'No.'

To ride in and out was not a startling idea. A man I knew well, an old Rhodesian, expected his servant to ride in five miles every morning to be there to get morning tea ready by six a.m.

'Just give him a chit to say he's working for you,' said my mother, who wanted to please her servant, Abraham, Benjamin or Moses.

'That would be breaking the law. Don't you care about that?'

'I sometimes think you deliberately do all you can to make things difficult for me,' said my mother.

By this time I was working part-time with a Mr Lamb. A Lord Milner had created a famous team of young men, called Milner's Kindergarten, to staff parts of the British Empire that might want clever, honest and highly trained young men. My Mr Lamb had been one. Now he was one of the shorthand writers for Hansard, and for parliamentary committees. Why had he come to be a shorthand writer after such a brilliant start? I never asked him. Now I would give a lot to know, but unfortunately, young, you omit to ask other people questions that only they can answer.

It was a pleasure to work for him. He was so clever, dry, ironical, and full of quips and quotations from his classical education.

But my mother went to see him to tell him that I was wrong-headed, and he ought to know whom he was employing.

Mr Lamb said to me, 'Your mother has been to see me, to say you are a danger and a threat to public order.'

I was angry, but what was the use of that?

'She says you are a Communist – but one of the advantages

of living in a goldfish bowl is that we all know about each other.'

'Well, I hardly keep it secret, Mr Lamb.'

'Precisely so. But it will probably infuriate you to know that we regard your current politics as an infantile disorder.'*

He twinkled triumph, and I had to laugh.

I tackled my mother. And when had that ever been of any use?

'Mother do you realize you could have lost me that job? And I earn more with him working odd hours than I did working in the office.'

Now she crumpled. She was suddenly flustered, guilty, and even panicked.

This complexity of emotions happens when a person has been mentally furious, full of rage at someone, attacking – mentally – some criminal or malicious enemy. But she was faced with just her daughter, an annoying, born-to-thwart-her girl whom it was her mission to save.

'Mother, that was a very wicked thing to do.'

'Oh, no, but he really did have to know. It was my duty ...'

If I met someone new, made a friend, even an acquaintance, she somehow got to know, and either made a friend of this person herself, or went to see them to say things about me, which, of course, were repeated back to me – and there was nothing I could do.

---

* Lenin once famously rebuked an inadequate young comrade, who planned extreme measures, saying that they were suffering from 'left-wing infantile disorders'.

'Mother, that wasn't very nice, was it?'

'But you are such a foolish, wrong-headed girl, somebody has to ...' Now I think this funny; then I felt as if I was caught in a spider's web.

And so the long, sad story went on. I always in flight from her, she always in pursuit.

I used to write down tales of mother-and-daughter enmities, and I had quite a collection.

These tales, summarized as a sentence, were dramatic enough. Expanded to a paragraph, they were elements of the absurd, of farce. Fleshed out to a page, what always became plain was a pitiful, improbable quality, as if this were a tale about freaks.

I shall write down here, just one, the simplest of these exemplary stories.

A mother and daughter did not 'get on'. Why did the girl not leave home? She stuck around, railing at her mother, but making use of any advantages, such as babysitting or handouts. Then her mother had a heart-attack, was helpless. The girl said to her, 'Very well, you've got me where you want me. I'll look after you but I shall never, ever say a word to you again.' And that was what happened. The mother lasted twenty years, and the daughter refused ever to say a syllable.

This is a quite mild story compared to some in my collection.

And then the war did end, it did, though sometimes we felt it would go on for ever. Had not wars done this in the past? And then it ended with those two bombs on Nagasaki and

Hiroshima, but at the time many of us could not see that these bombs were worse than what had already happened. Had we not already flattened the major cities of Japan? Which of course served it right for bombing Pearl Harbor. No, we were pleased the war had ended, it had actually ended … but then there was a post-war period and things did not seem much better. News was coming in of all kinds of horrors kept from us while the war went on. The concentration camps, for one. No, we did not at once 'take it in'. This news was too horrifying to 'take in', just like that: we needed time.

Our men had returned from fighting Rommel, those who did. There seemed more refugees every day, and soon they were from Stalin too, not only Hitler. Salisbury was crammed with the RAF wanting to go home. Some had been there for four, five years. The fliers and the bombers had been flown home, but the thousands of men who maintained the planes and the camps had to wait for the boats. The fitters and the turners and the riveters and engineers, the men who administered the camps, wanted just one thing: home, even if it was dark, cold, rationed.

In the room where there was a baby, much dandled and loved by young men who dreamed of family life, whose own lives had been on hold, I cooked for anything up to ten or more RAF most nights, bacon and eggs, sausages and baked beans, anything that my two hotplates could provide. They knew they were not going to be given plates of bacon and eggs at home when they did get there. Oh, when? They longed for the news that the troopships were at last available for them, but they certainly did not look forward to the actual journey. Every one of those young men said nothing could ever be worse than the voyage on the troopship out, from England to the ports of southern Africa – hell, they said it was – but it would be on those same ships they would go home: troopships that would not have been improved by their wartime experience.

I cooked. They ate. We were alike in just one thing: we were waiting for our real lives to begin. Now I would say we were like people recovering from an illness: we were numbed, stunned, because we hadn't really 'taken in' the years of war. For that matter I don't think the world has, even now, 'taken in' the war. In denial, are we? Yes. They may put on war films as often as they like, usually about the Nazis, but the whole world was at war, and whole areas of the conflict have hardly been looked at.

Meanwhile my mother was also feeding people: the RAF mostly.

My brother was back from the war, pretty deaf but whole, and still a bachelor. He met the RAF around and about the town and took them home to my mother's house where he was temporarily lodging. When I went to visit my mother in those days, her house was full of young men sitting about on the verandas, talking about what they would do when they did at last get home. She fed them, with the aid of her cookboy – the one who had wanted his brother to come and work for me. He was now living here, pretending to be invisible, illegal, but happy in town and not back in his village where nothing ever happened.

Those long afternoons that went on ... and on ... and on. To keep themselves awake after those vast meals, they sang, and soon my mother was at the piano, brought from the farm, still playable, though hardly pristine after years of rainy seasons when the keys swelled, the strings sagged, and the piano-tuner would say, 'I'm really sorry, but this is the best I can do.'

They sang the First World War songs, and if they did not know the words, my mother certainly did. 'Oh, oh, oh, what a lovely war' was a favourite because of the energetic tune, and so was 'Mademoiselle from Armentières'; and it often seemed the old piano would fly apart. The Second World War tunes, 'Well, I'm going to hang out my washing on the Siegfried Line', and 'Who do you think you are kidding, Mr Hitler?' – both with jolly tunes, and, very popular, 'Lili Marlene', German, which would lead to the current hits, of which one of the most popular, demanded by the young men again and again, was 'I'm gonna buy a Paper Doll that I can call my own, A doll the other fellows cannot steal ... When I come home at night she will be waiting, She'll be the truest doll in all the world ...'

Those young men had had girls when they left England, but they didn't have them now. Nor did they have girls here, in Africa. There were too many men, hundreds of thousands, in the various camps. They were forbidden to have relations with black women; and, anyway, there weren't enough of them either. No, those boys would have been lucky to have a paper doll, in those years. And they sang, over and over again, 'When I come home at night she will be waiting, She'll be the truest doll in all the world ...'

As the afternoon neared its end, 'We'll meet again, don't know where, don't know when ...' If you were a short way from the house looking out over the rise that soon would be carrying a new suburb, this song was unbearably sad, on and on, and then again, 'We'll meet again ... we'll meet again ...'

Quite soon my brother and I would pile our old cars with the young men and take them to town to catch their buses back to the camps, but meanwhile, even if it was the afternoon, they demanded to end with 'Goodnight, Sweetheart'.

Full daylight still, the street-lights not yet on, but,

Goodnight, Sweetheart,
Goodnight, Sweetheart,
Till we meet tomorrow,
Goodnight, Sweetheart,
Sleep will banish sorrow,
Tears and parting
May make us forlorn,
But with the dawn,
A new day is born,
So I'll say
Goodnight, Sweetheart ...

By the time they left my mother might have been playing

popular songs for hours – Emily McVeagh, who had once been told by her music teachers that she could have a career as a concert pianist if she wanted.

'She's a good sort,' said the RAF lads. 'She's a real sport, your mother.'

Those years before we all left Rhodesia, as ships became available, no, they were not a good time. You long for a war to end, and then it ends, and ... Sometimes, when life gets tough, I tell myself, 'If you could survive those years after the war, in Rhodesia, then you can survive anything.' I'm sure my mother wouldn't have much good to say about them. For one thing, both her children said to her, 'No, no, you will not run my life for me.'

'Anyone might think you were accusing me of being an interfering mother,' she cried, defiant, but humorous, because of the absurdity of it. There was even a roguish little twinkle, that begged me, my brother, to admit she was in the right, that what we had said was only a little fit of naughtiness. For a moment Emily McVeagh stood there, or perhaps even John McVeagh: I'm sure roguish twinkles were what he would go in for if unfairly accused.

I look back sometimes and see myself sitting on the steps of that house, listening to the thump-thump-thump of the jolly tunes, the wail of the sad ones, 'There is a long, long trail a-winding ...' and what I was thinking was, No, no, this is not possible.

The wireless is on, as always, telling us the news.

There are millions of refugees stumbling along bomb-cratered roads, starving, thirsty; there are thousands without homes; there is no harvest, no seeds to plant; in the ruins of Europe's great cities children are playing.

It could not be possible because every one of us had been brought up with 'Wash your hands before you sit down at table'; 'No, don't do that, or you'll tear your dress'; 'Please – you must say please and thank you'; 'A good little boy'; 'A bad little girl'; 'Be nice, Emma, Chantal, Hans, Dick, Ivan, Ingrid – you must be kind', all that, but still the bombs fell and ... some of these children brought up to expect law and order had heard bombs falling for four, five years. 'I simply cannot believe this isn't some awful dream.' So everyone, but everyone, was thinking, as we went through the war, the enormities of it, the weight of it, the horror of it, the grotesque nastiness of it all, This can't be happening, it can't ...

Along the veranda one of the young men is playing with my mother's little white dog, while still humming to the tunes, 'I'm gonna get a paper doll ...' He is bouncing a ball against a pillar and the dog is trying to catch it.

This young man, whose name I have forgotten, had had his own dog at home, but it had had to be put down: it was old, and its little stomach could not deal with the wartime food for animals. 'My mum did give him a little bit of her rations, but he was used to the best, my little dog was. His name was Patch, he had a black patch on an ear ...' He bounced the ball hard, and the little dog leaped. 'It's about time we left, isn't it? Goodnight, sweetheart, We'll meet again tomorrow ...' he sang to the dog.

The RAF did at last get home, and they wrote letters, we wrote letters, and my mother sold the house, when my brother married, and for the short years before she died, at seventy-three, she spent her afternoons and evenings playing bridge with other widows. She was, they all said, a very good bridge-player.

ACKNOWLEDGEMENTS

My thanks to the photographer Francesco Guidicini
who helped with some very old and sometimes
dilapidated photographs.